THE 1% PUSH LEGACY

The 1% Push Legacy

A Playbook for Leaders Who Win Through People, Not Just Performance

Nick Mornard

©2026 All Rights Reserved. No portion of this book may be reproduced, stored in a retrieval system, or transmitted in any form or by any means—electronic, mechanical, photocopy, recording, scanning, or other—except for brief quotations in critical reviews or articles without the prior permission of the author.

Published by Game Changer Publishing

Paperback ISBN: 979-8-90158-009-7

Hardcover ISBN: 979-8-90158-010-3

Digital ISBN: 979-8-90158-011-0

www.GameChangerPublishing.com

READ THIS FIRST

Just to say thanks for buying and reading my book,
I would like to connect!
Scan the QR Code Here:

THE 1% PUSH LEGACY

A PLAYBOOK FOR LEADERS WHO WIN THROUGH PEOPLE, NOT JUST PERFORMANCE

NICK MORNARD

CONTENTS

Introduction	ix
1. Leadership is a People Business	1
2. From Doing to Enabling: The Coach's Mindset	19
3. Trust: The Foundation of Growth	29
4. Positivity as a Competitive Advantage	39
5. Creating Your Leadership Playbook	49
6. The Art of the 1% Push in Daily Leadership	57
7. Accountability Without Fear	67
8. Empowerment in Action	75
9. The Ripple Effect of the 1% Push	83
10. Building a Culture of Continuous Improvement	91
11. Leading Through Change	97
12. The Leader's Mindset: Playing the Long Game	103
13. Developing Leaders Who Give the 1% Push	111
14. The Common Pitfalls of the 1% Push (and How to Avoid Them)	117
15. Your Leadership Legacy: Living the 1% Push	127
Your Push Starts Now	135
About the Author	137
Acknowledgments	139
The 1% Push Resources	141
Stay Connected With Nick	143
Also by Nick Mornard	145

INTRODUCTION
THE POWER OF A SMALL PUSH

My name is Nick Mornard, and my journey began on the hardwood floors of basketball courts across Europe. I lived my dream as a professional athlete, but even more importantly, I learned what it really takes to win in life. When I transitioned from basketball to business, it became clear that the same values applied: discipline, teamwork, resilience, and a strong mindset. Today I am a senior leader in a Fortune 500 company, a bestselling author, a leadership coach, and an entrepreneur building a growing travel agency team across the United States.

But those titles are not what define me. What truly defines me is purpose, growth, and helping others unlock their own potential.

When my playing days ended, there was no clear roadmap waiting for me. I had to start over. I stepped into new industries, faced setbacks, and constantly had to prove myself again. I was not always the most experienced or the most educated person in the room. What I did have was a commitment to show up, learn, improve, and push forward just a little more every single day. That mindset is what opened doors, earned trust, and created opportunities that changed my life.

INTRODUCTION

Eventually, I realized something important. Success in leadership is not about perfection. It comes from showing up with consistency and intention. It comes from pushing a little bit further every day, especially on the days when the push feels small. That is where the idea for The 1% Push Legacy began.

I wrote this book because I have seen so many talented people stop short of their potential. I have watched leaders burn out while trying to be perfect. I have watched teams fall apart because they lost sight of what leadership really is: people. I wanted to create something that brings together accountability and empathy, performance and humanity. Something that reminds leaders that they do not have to take giant leaps to create meaningful change. Small shifts can create big wins over time.

This book is for anyone who has ever felt stuck or overwhelmed by how far they think they have to go. It is for leaders who want to motivate, not intimidate. For entrepreneurs building from scratch. For people who know they are capable of more but are not sure where to start. If you have ever looked at someone successful and wondered how they keep going, this book will help you understand. It will help you build the mindset and habits that turn potential into real progress and real legacy, one day and one percent at a time.

Everything I share in these pages comes from experience. I have led high-performing teams through change, uncertainty, and growth. I have coached leaders who doubted themselves and watched them rise into positions they once thought were out of reach. I have failed, adapted, and rebuilt more times than I can count. Each time, setbacks taught me something new and prepared me for what came next. This is not a theory. It is a lived experience turned into actionable principles and practical steps.

Throughout this book, I will share the mindset, habits, and leadership principles behind The 1% Push. You will learn how to focus on progress instead of perfection, build trust and meaningful relationships, balance empathy and accountability, develop consistent habits that compound, and lead yourself in a way that allows you to lead

INTRODUCTION

others more effectively. This book is part playbook and part personal mirror. My hope is that as you read, you see your own ambition, your own spark, and your own story reflected in these pages.

More than anything, I hope this book reignites something inside you. I hope it reminds you that leadership is not about titles or popularity or being the loudest voice in the room. It is about how you show up, how you serve, and the influence you create when no one is watching. I hope this inspires you to push when you feel like pausing, to lead when you feel like stepping back, and to lift others even while you are still climbing.

One day, when you look back, I believe you will find that your legacy was not built in one big moment. It was built through small, consistent, intentional pushes that compounded over time. That is where greatness lives. Not in perfection, but in the push.

CHAPTER 1
LEADERSHIP IS A PEOPLE BUSINESS

When I think back to my days as a professional basketball player, the games we won were rarely about the flashiest plays or the most talented individual on the court. They were about the team: the way we communicated, trusted one another, and showed up for each other every single possession.

I still remember one game like it was yesterday, an away matchup where we were massive underdogs. Half our roster was out with injuries. The team we were about to face was taller, stronger, more talented, and operating on a budget that made ours look like pocket change. During warmups, I watched them run crisp, perfectly timed drills while their coaches barked instructions and fans filled the stands, confident and smiling.

Meanwhile, we were just seven players, two pulled up from the reserve squad and not even used to first-team minutes. Our warmup was simple: a few layups, some light shooting, quiet focus. On paper, we didn't stand a chance.

Then our coach gathered us in the locker room.

He didn't draw complex plays on the whiteboard or talk about strategy. He looked us in the eyes and said: "We may not have the most talent in this gym tonight, but we have each other. And if we play for one another, trust one another, and refuse to give up, we'll be the team that walks out of here proud."

It wasn't a tactical master class. It was a reminder of who we were: A group built on trust, discipline, and belief.

When we stepped onto the court, something shifted. Every player gave everything, diving for loose balls, rotating on defense, and cheering each other after every made shot. The energy was contagious. It didn't matter that they were bigger or faster—we played connected.

By the final buzzer, we'd done the unthinkable. We won by three points.

That victory sparked a long winning streak, not because we suddenly became more talented, but because we learned the true power of belief and unity.

That season opened my eyes to something I've carried ever since:

Mindset, consistency, and trust beat talent most of the time.

When a group commits to each other, when they push 1% harder every day, they become unstoppable.

The same is true in leadership. No matter how brilliant your strategy, innovative your technology, or ambitious your targets... your success will always come down to people.

I've led teams in high-pressure corporate environments, coached athletes, and worked with leaders across industries. And here's the universal truth I've seen: leadership is not a numbers game. It's a people game.

WHY PEOPLE COME FIRST

I still remember the day my coach pulled me aside after practice.

We had just finished one of those sessions that left everyone exhausted and ready to head home. I'd had a rough practice; my shots weren't falling, my energy was off, and I was frustrated. As the rest of the team filed out, I stayed behind, still shooting in silence, trying to find my rhythm again.

Coach walked over, picked up a loose ball, and passed it to me.

He didn't yell. He didn't blame me; he just said, "Nick, I don't need you to be perfect, I just need you to win one more rep than you lose."

That line hit me harder than any drill or conditioning session ever could.

He went on, "You'll have nights when nothing goes right. You'll miss shots. You'll make mistakes. But what separates good players from great ones is simple: they stay in the fight. They push when everyone else quits."

That moment changed how I approached everything, not just basketball, but life.

I realized that leadership, performance, and growth don't come from the highlight plays. They come from what happens after the frustration, when you decide to give one more push. That 1% effort, that one more shot, that one more conversation you didn't want to have, are the moments that compound into success.

Looking back, that coach wasn't just teaching me how to play better; he was teaching me how to lead myself. He was investing in me the way all great leaders do by seeing past the moment and helping me see what I could become.

Years later, when I found myself leading teams in business, I realized I was doing the same thing. Coaching others through their missed shots, their tough quarters, their "off days." Because the same truth applies: leaders don't build success; they build people who believe in their ability to push 1% further.

That's why I wrote this book. It's why I believe every small push matters.

And it's why I'll always be grateful for the coach who taught me that you don't have to be perfect to be great. You just have to keep pushing.

In sports, coaches spend countless hours scouting opponents, reviewing film, and drawing up plays. But the great ones spend just as much time, often more, understanding their players.

I remember one season early in my professional career when I couldn't seem to get out of my own head. My confidence had taken a hit from a few bad games in a row and missed shots I normally made, and I started to doubt myself. I showed up to practice every day, but I wasn't the same player. My energy was off. My body was there, but my mindset wasn't.

One afternoon, after a rough training, my coach pulled me aside as everyone headed to the locker room. He didn't start with stats or criticism. He just said, "Nick, I don't care about the shots you're missing. I care about the energy you're not giving."

Then he paused and added, "You're our natural leader. Don't let one bad week make you forget who you are."

He didn't yell. He didn't bench me. He invested in me. He saw that I didn't need correction; I needed belief.

The next day, he gave me a small but powerful assignment: to lead the pre-practice warm-up and talk to every player before we started. It wasn't about drills; it was about reconnecting with the team and rebuilding my confidence through purpose.

That one decision changed everything. Within a few weeks, my game came back, not because of new techniques, but because someone reminded me that my value was bigger than my performance.

That coach taught me something I've carried ever since: the best leaders see what people need before those people see it themselves. They coach the person, not just the player. They understand that confidence isn't a skill; it's an environment.

The best leaders know who needs encouragement after a mistake, who thrives under pressure, and who plays better when given space to figure things out. They know who has unshakable confidence and who is one bad day away from doubting themselves.

That underdog game wasn't won because of superior tactics or individual talent; it was won because our coach understood his players on a human level. He knew that no amount of whiteboard diagrams could replace belief. In that locker room, he read the moment perfectly.

He didn't talk about plays; he talked about people. He knew what we needed as a team: encouragement, confidence, and connection.

That moment was a master class in empathetic accountability, one of my key leadership strategies. It's the ability to push performance through people, not at them. Our coach held us accountable for effort and trust, but he did it with empathy and belief. He gave us ownership instead of control.

He didn't just say, "Play harder," He said, "Play for each other."

That simple shift created emotional investment, and that's what fueled the extra 1% from everyone on the floor.

Our coach saw beyond ability. He saw the mindset. He understood that every player is different.

Some need to be challenged to rise, some need to be encouraged to believe, and all need to feel trusted to perform.

By understanding what drives each individual, he built a collective confidence greater than any stat sheet or talent ranking. That's what leadership looks like; that's the 1% Push in action.

It's about leading people in a way that honors their differences, strengthens their belief, and unlocks performance through connection. When leaders see people, not just players, they build teams that don't just execute; they believe.

It's the same in business. Your team is made up of individuals with unique strengths, motivations, and challenges. If you don't know them, truly know them, you can't lead them effectively.

This isn't about "being nice" or having endless social lunches. It's about knowing what drives your people so you can set them up to deliver their best work.

A 2019 Gallup study found that employees who feel their manager knows them as a person are 27% more likely to be engaged in their work. Engagement isn't just about happiness. Engaged employees produce better results, innovate more, and stay longer.

THE TWO TYPES OF LEADERS

Over the years, I've noticed there are two types of leaders:

1. **Task-Centric Leaders** – They focus almost entirely on processes, KPIs, and output. People are "resources," not individuals.
2. **People-Centric Leaders** – They still care about results (deeply), but they know results are the byproduct of investing in their people first.

Task-centric leaders focus almost entirely on processes, KPIs, and output. They're driven by deadlines, metrics, and performance charts. Their intentions are good, and they want results, but their approach often misses the mark because it treats people as resources, not individuals.

In environments like that, performance becomes transactional: "Do this. Hit that target. Move faster."

It works in the short term, but it's unsustainable. People burn out. Creativity disappears. Engagement drops because the team no longer feels seen, only measured.

Sports Context: I once played for a coach who was obsessed with the scoreboard. Every practice was timed, every mistake stopped and analyzed, every possession tied to stats. We ran efficient systems, but the energy was flat. Players stopped taking risks because they were afraid to fail.

We executed plays perfectly, but we didn't believe it. When a team plays not to lose instead of playing to win, it's usually because the environment has become more about performance metrics than purpose.

Corporate Context: Years later, in my corporate career, I worked under a manager who measured everything: call times, response rates, weekly meetings, and nothing else. There were dashboards everywhere, but no connection. We hit numbers, but morale sank, and culture was lacking.

That experience reminded me that you can't measure trust or belief, yet those are the two things that sustain performance when times get tough.

Task-centric leaders get results, but only until people stop caring.

The second kind of leaders, people-centric leaders, care deeply about results too, but they understand that results are the byproduct of investing in their people first. They focus on trust, mindset, and growth because they know performance follows belief.

They ask: "How can I help you succeed?" not, "Why didn't you hit your target?"

They understand their people as individuals, what motivates them, what drains them, and how they respond to challenges. They don't lower expectations; they elevate people to meet them.

Sports Context: One of the best coaches I ever had pulled me aside after a tough loss. Instead of dissecting every mistake, he said, "You don't need to play harder. You need to trust your instincts again."

He didn't coach my mechanics; he coached my mindset. That one sentence reignited my confidence and changed how I showed up the rest of the season. He cared about the person

behind the player, and because of that, we all played better.

Corporate Context: When I stepped into leadership within a Fortune 500 organization, I made it my mission to embody that same approach. I focused on creating connections, talking with team members about their goals, their confidence, and their personal wins, not just their metrics.

When performance started slipping in one region, instead of adding pressure, I added presence. I met with the team, listened to their frustrations, and re-centered them on purpose. Within two months, the numbers rebounded, not because we changed the strategy, but because we rebuilt belief.

Task-centric leaders often see quick wins but struggle with long-term retention, culture, and innovation. People-centric leaders may take longer to build momentum, but once they do, the results are stronger, more sustainable, and achieved with less burnout.

On one of my previous teams, I watched a manager drive record-breaking quarterly numbers through constant pressure, daily check-ins, leaderboard rankings, and strict metrics. It worked... for a while. But within six months, turnover skyrocketed, creativity vanished, and the culture eroded.

Later, a new leader took over, one who focused on trust, coaching, and clarity instead of control. Progress was slower at first, but after a few months, the team's engagement and retention soared, and performance followed. That's when I realized: short-term speed can't compete with long-term stability built on belief.

A LESSON FROM THE LOCKER ROOM

In one of my final seasons playing pro basketball, I joined a team that was struggling badly. On paper, we had more than enough talent to win, but there was no chemistry, no connection. Players looked out for themselves, not each other.

I'll never forget one game when our lack of chemistry was on full display. Late in the fourth quarter, we were down by two with less than a minute left. Instead of running the play that the coach had drawn up, our point guard waved everyone off to take a contested shot on his own. He missed; no one boxed out, and the other team scored in transition. When the buzzer sounded, we didn't just lose the game; we walked off in silence, each player blaming someone else. That moment said it all: we had skill, but no trust, and honestly, no leadership... And without any of that, talent didn't matter.

Mid-season, our coach made a bold move. He called a meeting and said, "From now on, no one sits alone in the locker room. No one eats lunch alone. We're not just teammates. We're going to be a team."

At first, it felt forced. We had each other's backs. And by the end of the season, we went from the bottom of the standings to the playoffs. The coach had made us do team meetups, mandatory team dinners, and pre-practice huddles. Nobody loved it; we were frustrated, losing, and tired of being told we needed more "team chemistry," But little by little, something started to shift. Within weeks, something changed. We started talking more on the court. We celebrated small wins.

At the first few get-togethers, conversations were awkward: quick lunches, short talks, and everyone was guarded. But by the third or fourth time, walls started coming down. We started talking about life outside basketball, family, goals, and even funny travel stories from other leagues. We began realizing that the guys we barely spoke to outside the locker room were dealing with the same pressures, the same doubts, the same hunger to prove themselves.

Then came practice. One day, during a scrimmage, one of our rookies dove for a loose ball. Normally, that would have been a solo effort, the kind of thing nobody followed up on. But this time, two more guys hit the floor right after him. Everyone on the sideline erupted. It wasn't the play that mattered; it was the energy. That moment said, "we're in this together." From that day on, it spread. Players started helping each other off the floor. When someone missed a shot, you'd hear, "Keep shooting, we trust you, next one is in!" When a teammate got beaten on defense, another stepped up without hesitation, and rotations happened organically.

The culture flipped, not overnight but one small action at a time. By the end of the season, we went from the bottom of the standings to the playoffs. We weren't the most talented team, but we became the most connected. Every player had his teammates' backs, and trust turned effort into belief, and belief into wins.

That experience taught me something: you don't build winning teams through pressure; you build them through connection. When people know they're supported, they go above and beyond to win for each other.

What changed? Not the playbook. Not the drills. The relationships changed.

THE 1% PUSH IN PEOPLE-CENTRIC LEADERSHIP

Being a people-first leader doesn't mean you have to make massive, sweeping changes. Often, it's the small, consistent gestures, the 1% Push, that create the biggest shifts.

Here are a few examples:

- Taking two extra minutes after a meeting to recognize someone's contribution.
- Asking a team member how they're doing and actually listening to the answer.
- Giving someone the space to lead a small project to build their confidence.
- Checking in on someone outside of a work issue, simply because you care.

Individually, these actions might feel insignificant. But over time, they build trust, connection, and motivation. Just like a basketball team that practices the fundamentals day after day, these habits create a foundation for winning.

Being a people-first leader doesn't mean reinventing your organization or overhauling every process overnight. It's not about grand gestures or sweeping cultural shifts. Most of the time, it's the 1% small, intentional actions repeated with consistency that change everything. The 1% Push is the daily decision to invest just a little more attention, energy, or care into someone than you did yesterday. Those moments compound.

I've seen it firsthand. After one particularly intense quarter, I took two extra minutes at the end of a team meeting to call out a partner who had caught an error that saved a client relationship. Her face lit up. That simple recognition, a micro-moment of appreciation, triggered something powerful: psychological validation. People crave to be seen, and when they feel noticed, their engagement skyrockets.

Another time, I asked a team member how he was doing. Not the usual "How's everything?" on the way to the next call, but a real question with space for a real answer. He opened up about burnout I hadn't noticed. Just listening, without trying to fix, I built psychological safety, showing him that his value wasn't tied to his output alone. Within weeks, his energy and creativity came back stronger than ever.

Then there was a newer associate who lacked confidence but had strong ideas. I gave her a small project to lead. It wasn't high-risk, but it was high-trust. Watching her grow into the role reminded me of a truth I first learned in basketball: people rise when they're trusted with responsibility. That's autonomy in action, and it creates ownership far deeper than any motivational speech ever could.

Sometimes the most impactful 1% Push isn't about performance at all. I've texted team members after tough days just to check in; no agenda, no ask. Those small gestures communicate belonging, the emotional bond that turns a group of individuals into a team.

Individually, these actions might seem insignificant. But just like a basketball team that practices layups, defense, and communication every single day, these small pushes form the muscle memory of trust. Over time, they build a foundation for connection, confidence, and commitment, the true ingredients of sustained performance.

That's the power of the 1% Push. It's not about doing everything differently; it's about doing the right small things consistently until they transform the culture around you.

STORY FROM THE BOARDROOM

Years later, in a corporate setting, I was leading an underperforming regional division. Upper management's instinct was to increase reporting, tighten controls, and demand more output.

Instead, I did something different. I visited every team in person and asked one question: "What's one thing we can change to make your job easier?"

One conversation still stands out. During one of those visits, a team member mentioned that their biggest frustration wasn't workload; it was time wasted waiting for internal approvals that could easily be automated. It was a small operational detail I'd never noticed. Within a week, we streamlined the process. That single change saved hours every week, but more importantly, it sent a message: their voice mattered. Productivity improved, yes, but so did trust. People started speaking up more and sharing ideas freely because they saw that even a small suggestion could spark a big difference.

Some answers were small, like fixing a reporting tool that froze constantly. Others were bigger, like streamlining a cumbersome approval process. But what happened was bigger than any single fix: people saw that I cared.

Within months, performance started to rise. Not because I imposed more pressure, but because people felt heard and respected. The more they trusted me, the harder they worked for themselves, their teams, and the mission.

One associate started completely disengaged; she was smart, capable, but clearly checked out. During a one-on-one, we sat down for a short conversation that had nothing to do with KPIs or performance. I just asked about her goals, what motivated her, and what she actually wanted out of her career. A few weeks later, she approached me with an idea to improve how we supported our clients. We tested it and it worked. Within months, she became one of the top performers on the team. That's when it clicked: people don't buy into companies, they buy into relationships. When someone feels seen, they start showing up not because they have to, but because they want to.

A PRACTICAL FRAMEWORK: THE CARE MODEL

One tool I often share with leaders who want to be more people-focused is the CARE Model:

- **C – Connect:** Learn about your team members as individuals, not just their job titles. Example: Have one meaningful, non-work conversation with each direct report every month.
- **A – Acknowledge:** Recognize effort, not just outcomes. Effort shows commitment; results follow. Example: Celebrate small wins publicly, not just big ones.
- **R – Respect:** Give people autonomy and treat their ideas as valuable. Example: In meetings, don't just ask for input; ask specific people for their thoughts.
- **E – Empower:** Provide opportunities for growth, even if it means stretching comfort zones. Example: Assign stretch projects with clear support but minimal micromanagement.

For me, CARE isn't a checklist; it's a rhythm I try to live as a leader.

Connect: I make it a priority to have real conversations beyond the numbers. I remember flying out to visit one of our regional teams and sitting down with an associate who seemed quiet in meetings. We ended up talking about her kids' college search for twenty minutes. That simple conversation changed everything. She started speaking up more, leading projects, and mentoring others.

Acknowledge: Recognition doesn't have to wait for a big win. After a tough quarter, I once sent a short email to highlight a team member who had gone above and beyond for a client. It took me two minutes, but that moment of acknowledgment boosted not only her confidence but also lifted the entire team's morale.

Respect: In meetings, I make it a point to invite perspectives, not just data. I once turned to a quiet but sharp project leader and asked for her view on a strategic decision. Her insight reshaped our approach and reminded the team that respect means creating space for every voice, not just the loudest ones.

Empower: I believe growth happens when people are trusted with responsibility. One of my proudest moments as a leader was watching a newer associate I'd given a stretch project to, something just beyond her comfort zone, completely own it. I provided guidance when needed but stayed out of the way. She delivered exceptional results and earned her first promotion shortly after.

Those moments, small, consistent, intentional, are what the CARE Model is really about. When people feel connected, acknowledged, respected, and empowered, they don't just perform, they thrive.

THE ROI OF PUTTING PEOPLE FIRST

Some leaders still view "people-first" leadership as soft, but the numbers tell a different story. According to Gallup's 2018 research, companies with high employee engagement are 21% more profitable. Likewise, a 2022 *Forbes* analysis highlighted that teams who feel valued experience 59% lower turnover, as reported by the Work Institute. McKinsey reports that leaders rated highest in people skills consistently outperform financially (McKinsey & Company, 2022).

I've seen both sides of that equation. Early in my corporate career, I worked under a leader who focused solely on metrics: calls, conversions, and charts. We hit short-term goals, but morale dropped, innovation stalled, and within a year, half the team left. Later, I led a team where I flipped that approach: putting trust, recognition, and growth first. It didn't change results overnight, but within months, performance rose and turnover fell.

That's when I learned what the data proves: people-first leadership isn't soft; it's smart business. When people feel seen and supported, they don't just work harder; they work with purpose.

The bottom line: focusing on people is not a trade-off with performance; it's the driver of performance.

THE DANGER OF NEGLECT

On the flip side, leaders who ignore the human side of leadership often pay the price in hidden costs:

- High turnover (which is expensive: replacing an employee can cost up to twice their salary).
- Low engagement (which drags down productivity).
- Burnout (which quietly erodes both morale and output).

In sports, if a player feels unseen or undervalued, they eventually stop giving 100%. In business, it's no different.

I saw it happen once with a talented teammate early in my career. He was one of the hardest workers on the team, always early to practice, always pushing others, but he rarely got recognition. When plays went well, others got the spotlight; when things went wrong, he got the criticism. Over time, his energy changed. He stopped diving for loose balls, stopped talking on defense, and stopped caring. He didn't lose skill; he lost the belief that his effort mattered.

I've seen the same thing in business. When people feel unseen or undervalued, they stop bringing their best ideas, their extra effort, their passion. It's not about ability, it's about acknowledgment. Recognition doesn't cost anything, but the absence of it can cost everything.

> **LOCKER ROOM LESSON**
> *People don't give their best to leaders they fear.*
> *They give their best to leaders they trust.*

REFLECTION QUESTIONS

1. How well do you know the personal goals and motivations of your team members?
2. When was the last time you acknowledged effort, not just results?
3. Which relationships in your team could benefit from a 1% Push this week?

ACTION STEPS

- This week, schedule at least one non-transactional conversation with a team member without project updates, just connection.
- Pick one team member and give them ownership of a small but meaningful task.
- Send a genuine note of appreciation to someone for the way they approached a challenge, not just the outcome.

REAL LIFE STORY: THE ROOKIE WHO CHANGED THE GAME

On one of the teams I played on, our roster included a rookie named Thomas. He wasn't the tallest, the fastest, or the most naturally gifted player; in fact, he barely made the team. On paper, he was average.

But our head coach saw something that no stat sheet could capture. He saw potential.

Instead of just telling Thomas to "work harder" or benching him when he struggled, the coach invested in him with small "pushes" every day. After practice, the coach would pull Thomas aside to work on a single skill: not ten things, not everything he needed to fix, just one small improvement each day. One day it was footwork, the next it was shooting form, then defensive positioning. I still remember his first practice, nerves everywhere, missing layups, fumbling passes, but the coach never flinched. He just said, "We'll fix one thing at a time."

At first, it didn't look like much was changing. But week after week, those micro-improvements stacked up. Six months later, Thomas was not only in the starting lineup, but he was also one of the most reliable players in critical moments. In one playoff game, Thomas made the critical play, a perfectly timed steal in the final seconds that sealed the win. That moment didn't come from luck; it came from months of small, intentional growth.

THE LEADERSHIP LESSON

When I later transitioned into corporate leadership, I realized, in sports, you're not coaching positions; you're coaching people.

In business, you're not managing job descriptions; you're leading human beings.

What transformed Thomas wasn't a playbook, a spreadsheet, or a motivational speech. It was a consistent belief, targeted feedback, and the discipline to focus on people over process.

> *"People buy into the leader before they buy into the vision"*
> —John C. Maxwell

TAKEAWAY FOR LEADERS

Leadership is a people business. Titles, processes, and KPIs are important, but they don't inspire loyalty or unlock someone's true potential. People follow leaders who see them, believe in them, and push them, even if it's just 1% more, toward the best version of themselves.

Key Takeaway: Leadership is and will always be about people. The processes matter. The metrics matter. But without strong relationships and a people-first mindset, none of it will last.

CHAPTER 2

FROM DOING TO ENABLING: THE COACH'S MINDSET

When I transitioned from being a professional basketball player to leading teams in the corporate world, I learned a hard truth: my instinct to "jump in and make the play" didn't serve me anymore.

When I first moved into leadership, I treated business like basketball; if something was off, I jumped in to fix it. During one client presentation, a newer team member started struggling through her section, and my instinct kicked in. I stepped in, took over, and got the deal across the finish line, but afterward, I realized I'd taken her opportunity to grow.

She didn't need me to make the play; she needed me to coach her through it. That moment taught me one of my most important leadership lessons: sometimes the best way to lead is to step back, not step in.

On the court, if the game was on the line and I had the ball, I knew I could take the shot. In business, however, leadership isn't about taking the shot yourself. It's about making sure the right person is ready and confident to take it.

The best leaders understand they're no longer the star player; they're the coach. And the coach's job is not to rack up personal stats. It's to create the conditions for others to succeed.

THE TRAP OF THE STAR PLAYER

Many leaders struggle with this shift. They were promoted because they were great individual contributors: the top salesperson, the best project manager, or the go-to problem solver. So, when pressure hits, they default to what worked before: doing it themselves.

The problem? When you're doing the work for your team, you're robbing them of the opportunity to grow. You might solve today's problem faster, but you're slowing down tomorrow's progress.

A LESSON FROM MY PLAYING DAYS

I remember a game early in my career when our starting point guard got injured in the second quarter. I was used to playing forward, but the coach moved me into his position. When you play a specific position in basketball, you learn during practices how to run those plays, and it becomes automatic. The problem is that when you suddenly have to play another position, you have to think through the plays, and I was a step late. I made mistakes setting the wrong screens. I wasn't ready. I made mistakes. I turned the ball over.

But here's what I remember most: the coach didn't pull me out. He pulled me aside, gave me a quick tip, and said, "You've got this. I believe in you." This reinforced my confidence.

We ended up winning that game, but more importantly, I walked away with a new skill and new confidence. That's what enabling looks like: trusting someone enough to let them learn in real time.

DOING VS. ENABLING: THE CORE DIFFERENCES	
Doing	Enabling
Focuses on personal execution	Focuses on team capability
Solves the problem yourself	Guides others to solve it
Creates dependency	Builds independence
Short-term win	Long-term growth
"I'll handle it"	"How will you handle it?"

DOING VS. ENABLING: THE CORE DIFFERENCES

WHY LEADERS STRUGGLE TO LET GO

If you've been in a high-performance role before becoming a leader, it's natural to want to keep your hands in everything. The challenges are:

- **Fear of mistakes:** "If I don't do it, it might get messed up."
- **Pride in skill:** "I'm still the best at this, so I should do it."
- **Pressure for speed:** "It's faster if I just handle it."

But here's the leadership truth: If everything still depends on you, you haven't built a team; you've built a bottleneck.

THE 1% PUSH IN THE COACH'S MINDSET

Shifting from doing to enabling isn't a single leap. It's a series of small pushes in how you lead every day:

- Ask: "What's your plan?" instead of "Here's what you should do."
- Give someone ownership of a project you'd normally handle yourself.

- Let a team member lead a meeting while you observe and support.
- Step back during problem-solving sessions and resist the urge to jump in with the answer.

Each time you give space instead of taking over, you're giving a *1% Push* toward their growth and confidence.

A CORPORATE STORY

When I was leading a strategic initiative in my corporate role, a critical client presentation was coming up. I had delivered hundreds of these, and my natural instinct was to take the lead.

Instead, I assigned it to one of my emerging leaders. I coached her through the preparation, reviewed her slides, and practiced Q&A with her, but I didn't take the stage.

When I was leading a strategic client retention initiative for our region, we had a critical presentation with one of our largest accounts, a deal worth millions in annual revenue. Normally, I would've led it myself; I'd done it numerous times before. But this time, I handed it to one of my emerging leaders. She'd shown strong analytical skills and genuine curiosity about client strategy, and I wanted her to step into the spotlight.

At first, she was nervous, questioning whether she was ready, but we worked through it together. I coached her on structure, reviewed her slides, and ran practice sessions. When the day came, she delivered with confidence and authenticity. The client renewed their contract, but the real win was watching her realize she didn't just belong in the room; she could lead it.

She nailed it. The client loved her energy, and she gained instant credibility across the team. That single opportunity accelerated her career more than a year's worth of standard assignments could have.

That moment paid dividends in more ways than one. By stepping back, I gained something every leader needs: trust and leverage. The team saw that I wasn't just talking about empowerment; I was living it. That built confidence, loyalty, and initiative across the board.

For me personally, it was a turning point. I realized that my success as a leader wouldn't be measured by how many presentations I could deliver, but by how many leaders I could develop. That single decision multiplied my impact and freed me to focus on vision, strategy, and growth instead of being the one always making the play.

FRAMEWORK: THE COACH MODEL FOR ENABLING LEADERSHIP

- **C – Clarify the Goal:** Make sure your team member knows exactly what success looks like. When people know the target, they can take full ownership of hitting it. Desired Outcome: Aligned expectations and accountability. Everyone knows the "why" and the "what." Example: "By Friday, we need a proposal that answers these three client questions."
- **O – Offer Resources:** Give your team the tools, contacts, and context they need to succeed. Empowerment without resources is just pressure. Desired Outcome: Reduced friction, higher confidence, and faster progress.
- **A – Ask, Don't Answer:** Guide with questions instead of instructions. When you ask, "What's your plan to approach this?" you're building problem solvers, not order takers. Desired Outcome: Independent thinkers who grow in confidence and creativity. Example: "What's your plan to approach this?" instead of "Here's what to do."
- **C – Check In (without taking over):** Offer support and feedback at key checkpoints, but resist the urge to jump in. Trust is built through presence, not control. Desired Outcome: Sustained momentum, stronger trust, and true accountability.

- **H – Highlight Wins:** Publicly recognize effort and progress, not just final results. Small wins compound into big victories. Desired Outcome: A motivated, engaged team fueled by confidence and continuous improvement.

The COACH Model works because it shifts leadership from control to collaboration. Each step is designed to meet the psychological and performance needs that drive human motivation, clarity, autonomy, support, and recognition.

This is how sports dynasties are built. The coach invests in every player's growth so the team can succeed no matter who's on the floor. And when business leaders coach, they multiply their impact. The COACH Model doesn't just improve performance; it creates leaders who can perform without constant supervision, which is the real win.

THE LONG-TERM PAYOFF

When you enable instead of doing, you:

- Build leaders, not followers.
- Free yourself to focus on strategy, not firefighting.
- Create a culture of ownership where people step up without being asked.

LOCKER ROOM LESSON
Your role as a leader isn't to be the best player on the team.
It's to make everyone else better.

REFLECTION QUESTIONS

1. Where are you still acting like the star player instead of the coach?
2. What's one task or project you could hand over this week to help someone else grow?
3. How comfortable are you with letting your team make mistakes as part of their learning?

ACTION STEPS

- Identify one recurring task you currently own and assign it to a capable team member this week.
- Schedule a coaching session to prepare them for success.
- After they complete their task, review together what worked and what could be improved, and then step back again next time.

REAL LIFE STORY: THE GAME I DIDN'T PLAY

Early in my basketball career, I had a coach who loved to do everything himself. He'd run the warm-ups, demonstrate every drill, even step into scrimmages to "show us how it's done." We respected his skills, but here's the problem: when game day came, he wasn't on the court with us.

I remember one close game where that approach really cost us. Late in the fourth quarter, we were down by two, and the play our coach called was one he always ran himself in practice. The problem was, none of us had ever actually executed it under pressure; he'd always been the one demonstrating. When the moment came, we hesitated, missed our spacing, and turned the ball over.

After the loss, it hit me: our coach had trained us to watch, not to lead. His need to do everything himself left us unprepared when it mattered most.

Later in my career, I played under a different coach who rarely touched the ball in practice. Instead, he stood on the sideline, watching closely. He wasn't there to do the work. He was there to make sure we could do it. His job was to prepare us, to create scenarios, to challenge us in ways that mirrored the pressure of real competition.

In one tight playoff game, we were down by three with seconds left. During the timeout, he didn't draw up a flashy new play. He looked at me and simply said, "You've done this in practice a hundred times. You know what to do." And we did. We tied it up and won in overtime.

THE LEADERSHIP LESSON

That night wasn't won because the coach made the shot. It was won because weeks earlier, he'd shifted his mindset from doing to enabling. He gave us the tools, the confidence, and the decision-making skills to perform without him on the court.

> *"Leaders don't win games by taking the shot.*
> *They win by preparing others to take it."*

TAKEAWAY FOR LEADERS

The real victory is when your people perform at their best without you feeling the need to step in.

Key Takeaway: The measure of your leadership isn't what you achieve personally. It's what your team achieves because of you. Shift from doing to enabling, and you'll build not just results, but leaders.

CHAPTER 3
TRUST: THE FOUNDATION OF GROWTH

In every championship team I've ever been part of, whether on the basketball court or in the boardroom, there was one constant: trust.

On the court, I learned the power of trust the hard way. During one playoff run, I wasn't the leading scorer; my role was defense and facilitating. In one game, with seconds left, I passed up a decent shot to hit a teammate in the corner. He drained it. That moment taught me that trust isn't just belief in others; it's the willingness to rely on them when it counts.

Years later, in business, I felt the same thing during a major client renewal. A tight deadline, high stakes, my instinct was to take control. Instead, I trusted my team to lead their sections. They delivered flawlessly, and the client not only renewed but expanded the partnership.

In both arenas, the lesson was identical: trust is the bridge between preparation and performance. When you trust people, they don't just execute; they elevate.

Trust isn't a "nice to have" in leadership. It's the foundation on which everything else is built. You can have the perfect strategy, cutting-edge tools, and a talented roster, but without trust, the structure collapses. People won't take risks, speak up, or stretch beyond their comfort zones if they don't feel secure.

And here's the reality: trust doesn't just happen because you have a title. It's earned, and it's earned in small, consistent actions over time.

WHY TRUST MATTERS MORE THAN TALENT

I've seen incredibly talented teams fail because they didn't trust each other or their leader. And I've seen average teams outperform expectations because they trusted the process, the plan, and the person leading them.

I once played on a team stacked with talent, shooters, size, depth, everything you'd want on paper, but the locker room was divided. Players questioned every decision, blamed each other after losses, and tuned out the coach. We had the skill to win the league, but we couldn't get past the semifinals.

A few years later, I joined a smaller club that didn't have nearly the same talent, but the difference was night and day. Everyone bought into the system, trusted the coach, and trusted each other. No egos, no second-guessing, just commitment. We communicated, covered for each other, and executed without hesitation. That team overachieved, not because we were better players, but because we were a better team.

That experience taught me a simple truth I've carried into leadership ever since: trust beats talent when talent doesn't trust.

Trust transforms a group of individuals into a cohesive unit. It gives people the confidence to try, knowing their leader has their back, and the courage to hold each other accountable without fear of blame or politics.

A 2022 Harvard Business Review study found that employees in high-trust companies report 74% less stress, 50% higher productivity, and 76% more engagement. Trust doesn't just feel good; it's a performance multiplier.

INTRODUCING TBVA – TRUST-BASED, VALUE-ADDED

A couple of weeks ago, I spoke to a group of over 200 service professionals about a principle I live by: TBVA (Trust-Based Value-Added). The idea is simple but powerful.

1. **Trust-Based** – Everything begins with trust. Without it, nothing you say or do will land the way you want it to. People follow leaders they trust, not just because of their title, but because of their consistency, integrity, and authenticity.

I've experienced both sides of what trust can do and what happens when it's missing.

Early in my playing career, I was on a team where the coach constantly changed lineups, second-guessed players during games, and called out mistakes publicly. It wasn't that he didn't know basketball; he just didn't trust us to execute. And in return, we stopped trusting him. Players hesitated, played tight, and started looking out for themselves. By midseason, we weren't losing because of talent; we were losing because we were disconnected.

Years later, in my corporate role, I saw the opposite. I once led a project where the team faced tight deadlines and shifting priorities. Instead of micromanaging, I was transparent about challenges and trusted each person to own their part. When mistakes happened, we fixed them together with no blame, just accountability. That trust created a ripple effect: people communicated more, took initiative, and delivered faster than expected.

Those experiences cemented one of my core beliefs: trust isn't given by position; it's earned by consistency. When people trust your word, they'll follow your lead even through uncertainty. Without it, even the best strategy will fall flat.

2. **Value-Added** – Every interaction should leave the other person better than you found them. It could be a solution, a new perspective, encouragement, or even constructive feedback that helps them grow.

Trust gets you in the door, but value keeps you in the room. You may earn someone's trust once, but if you're not consistently adding value, that trust will fade, and so will the relationship.

The leadership lesson is that trust is what earns you the opportunity, opens doors, creates relationships, and gives you a chance to lead, but once you're in the room, value is what sustains that trust.

In leadership, that means showing up consistently with purpose, insight, and follow-through. People may initially believe in your character, but they'll stay aligned because of your contribution.

Trust gets people to listen, and value makes them want to keep listening. The best leaders understand that credibility isn't permanent; it's renewed every day through the impact you bring to others.

In short: trust starts the conversation; value earns you the right to continue it.

THE SILENT KILLER OF TRUST

One of the quickest ways to destroy trust is the gap between expectation and action. When you say one thing but do another or fail to follow through, that gap becomes the breeding ground for doubt, frustration, and disengagement.

That gap is where trust goes to die.

And once trust dies, you can rebuild it, but it takes far more time, effort, and transparency than it would have taken to maintain it in the first place.

I once worked under a manager who constantly preached "work-life balance." He said all the right things and encouraged us to take breaks, protect our time, and prioritize well-being. But when someone actually logged off on time, he'd message them an hour later asking for updates. Nobody said it out loud, but the message was clear: what he said and what he did didn't match.

Within months, trust evaporated. People stopped believing his words, and even genuine efforts to support the team were met with skepticism. It took a long time and a lot of humility on his part to rebuild that credibility.

That experience stuck with me. I learned that consistency is the currency of trust. It's not the promises that define your leadership; it's whether your actions prove them true.

THREE ELEMENTS OF TRUST

Over the years, I've found that trust in leadership comes down to three key elements:

1. **Transparency** – Share the "why" behind decisions, not just the "what." When your team understands the reasoning, they feel included and respected.
2. **Consistency** – Show up the same way, day after day. Be steady in your values, expectations, and how you treat people.
3. **Vulnerability** – Admit when you don't have all the answers. Owning your humanity builds connection, not weakness.

THE 1% PUSH IN BUILDING TRUST

Trust isn't built in grand gestures; it's built in small, everyday actions: following through on what you said you'd do, admitting mistakes quickly instead of covering them up, and being willing to have honest conversations even when they're uncomfortable. Think of each of these as small deposits in a trust bank account. Every consistent action strengthens the relationship, while every broken promise is a withdrawal. As with banking, it's much easier to maintain a healthy balance with steady deposits than to recover from an overdraft.

STORY FROM THE LOCKER ROOM

In Belgium, I remember one week when our coach told us we'd switch to a zone defense to counter a stronger inside team. We practiced it once and never used it again. In the next game, we got crushed in the paint, and nobody was surprised. Another time, he promised extra free-throw sessions after we lost two close games at the line, but he canceled for a sponsor event. Each broken promise chipped away at trust until we stopped believing what he said.

Later in my career, I had a coach who was the complete opposite. If he said we'd have a two-hour-long practice, that's exactly what happened. If he promised rest, he made sure we got it. Even when the message was tough, we knew it was real. That predictability built respect, and that respect fueled effort.

A CORPORATE STORY

In my corporate leadership role, I once inherited a team that had been through four managers in two years. Morale was low, and turnover was high. The feedback I kept hearing was, "We never know where we stand. Leaders say one thing and do another."

I knew I could not change that overnight, so I focused on small trust-building actions. If I promised to get back to someone by Friday, I followed up by Thursday. If I did not know the answer, I admitted it and committed to finding out. If we made a decision, we stuck with it unless there was a clear reason to change course, and when we did, I explained why.

Within six months, engagement scores rose and voluntary turnover dropped sharply. It was not because every process had been fixed, but because people finally believed what their leader said.

FRAMEWORK: THE TRUST LADDER

Here's a simple framework for thinking about trust in leadership:

1. **T – Tell the Truth:** Always start with honesty, even when it's uncomfortable.
2. **R – Respect Commitments:** Do what you say you'll do.
3. **U – Understand Others:** Listen deeply to your team's concerns and perspectives.
4. **S – Show Consistency:** Be predictable in your values and behavior.
5. **T – Take Responsibility:** Own mistakes and make them right.

Climb this ladder daily, and you'll build trust faster than you think. Skip a rung, and you risk slipping back down.

> **LOCKER ROOM LESSON**
> *Trust is built in drops and lost in buckets.*

REFLECTION QUESTIONS

1. Where might there be a gap between your words and actions right now?
2. Are you adding value in every interaction with your team, or are some touchpoints purely transactional?
3. How consistent are you in how you show up, not just when things are good, but when they're tough?

ACTION STEPS

- Identify one small promise you can make and keep this week to a team member.
- In your next team meeting, share the "why" behind one decision you've made.
- Audit your recent interactions: Did each one add value, or could you have done more?

REAL LIFE STORY: THE CLIENT WHO TESTED MY PATIENCE

Early in my corporate career, I worked with a major client who was, frankly, impossible to please. Every meeting felt like a battle. They questioned every recommendation, delayed approvals, and seemed skeptical of everything we presented.

One day, after another tense call, I decided to shift my approach. Instead of leading with deliverables, I started leading with trust. I made it a point to consistently show up prepared, follow through on every single commitment (no matter how small), and communicate with complete transparency, even when the news wasn't good.

It didn't change overnight. But slowly, they started to open up. Our conversations shifted from defensive to collaborative. They began to share more about their challenges, giving me insight to provide real value rather than just meeting contract terms.

At first, every meeting with that client felt tense: short answers, crossed arms, and constant pushback. After I changed my approach, the first sign of progress came a few weeks later when they actually replied, "Thanks for the quick turnaround," in an email, something they'd never done before. A month after that, they invited me to a planning session they'd previously kept internal.

By the end of the quarter, the same client who once challenged every slide was calling for my input before major decisions. What changed wasn't the product; it was the partnership. Consistency and honesty turned friction into collaboration, and that account eventually became one of our strongest long-term relationships.

Six months later, the same client who had once been a source of stress renewed their partnership for three years and sent me a handwritten note thanking me for finally making it feel like we were on the same team.

THE LEADERSHIP LESSON

That experience cemented two truths for me:

1. Trust gets you in the door, but value keeps you in the room.
2. The gap between expectation and action is where trust goes to die.

Trust isn't built in grand gestures. It's built in the tiny, consistent actions that prove your word means something.

TAKEAWAY FOR LEADERS

In business and in life, growth doesn't happen in an environment of suspicion or fear. If you want your team or clients to take bold steps, they have to believe you'll have their back, even if they stumble. Trust is the foundation that makes the 1% Push possible.

Key Takeaway: Trust is the foundation of leadership. It's what gets you in the door, but value is what keeps you in the room. Protect it fiercely, because once it's gone, everything else gets harder.

CHAPTER 4
POSITIVITY AS A COMPETITIVE ADVANTAGE

When I say "positivity," some leaders immediately think of sugarcoating reality, ignoring problems, or plastering on a fake smile when things are falling apart. That's not what I'm talking about.

One season, we were on a brutal losing streak; injuries, travel fatigue, and close losses were piling up. The locker room was heavy; everyone was frustrated. But there was one teammate, our backup point guard, who never stopped bringing energy. He wasn't our star or captain; he barely played ten minutes a game, but every day, he showed up smiling, cracking jokes, hyping guys up during warmups, and celebrating every made shot like it was a championship winner.

One night, after a particularly tough loss, he gathered us in the locker room and said, "We can't control the scoreboard, but we can control our spirit." Simple words, but it flipped something. The next game, our energy was different, more connected, more alive. We won, and that spark carried into a winning streak that turned our season around.

That teammate taught me something I've never forgotten: positivity is a performance multiplier. You don't need a title to lead; sometimes the loudest impact comes from the quietest encouragement.

In leadership, positivity is not about pretending everything is fine. It's about creating a belief that things can be better. It's the choice to approach challenges with solutions-focused thinking and to model resilience so your team feels safe pushing forward.

I've seen teams turn around games, seasons, and entire companies, not because they suddenly became more talented, but because they shifted their mindset from defeat to determination. That's the real competitive advantage of positivity.

WHY POSITIVITY IS A LEADERSHIP MULTIPLIER

The best leaders I've worked with share a common skill: they can walk into a room full of tension and replace fear with focus. They don't ignore problems; they reframe them as opportunities for growth.

There's science behind it: Barbara Fredrickson's broaden-and-build theory of positive emotions shows that positivity widens our range of thinking, helping us see more options and think more creatively. A 2021 Gallup study found that teams with leaders who demonstrate optimism are 31% more productive and have 23% higher engagement. In sports, we call this momentum. When a team believes it can win, it plays differently: faster, smarter, and more connected. In business, momentum is the same thing; it's belief in action.

A GAME THAT CHANGED EVERYTHING

I'll never forget a playoff game in which my team was being completely outplayed in the first half. Everything that could go wrong did. We missed open shots, turned the ball over, and gave up three straight fast breaks that silenced our bench. Their crowd was loud, their confidence growing with every basket. By the end of the second quarter, we looked defeated, heads down, no communication, guys arguing over missed assignments. I remember one play where two of our defenders went for the same rebound, collided, and the other team scored an easy putback. It summed up the half: effort without unity.

We went into the locker room down eighteen points. The room was tense. You could see it on everyone's faces: We're done. It was dead quiet, the kind of silence that feels heavier than shouting. No one made eye contact.

Our coach walked in, clapped his hands, and said, "Perfect. We've seen their best. Now they get to see ours." He didn't deny the score. He didn't give a thirty-minute lecture. He reframed the situation in one sentence.

We came out of that tunnel with different energy. The same players who were slumped minutes earlier were now diving for loose balls and high-fiving after every stop. The scoreboard hadn't changed yet, but we had. Every possession felt like a fresh chance to shift the game. And we did, slowly chipping away until we won in the final minute.

That's what positivity does: it changes the energy in the room, which changes the behavior on the floor.

THE 1% PUSH IN POSITIVITY

You don't need a locker room speech every day to lead with positivity. In fact, the most powerful form of positivity is delivered in small, consistent pushes. Start a meeting by recognizing someone's effort, even if the results aren't in yet. Frame setbacks as lessons: "What did we learn?" instead of "Why did we fail?" Use "we" instead of "you" when addressing challenges.

These micro-moments accumulate, creating an environment where people feel safe taking risks, speaking up, and keep going even when the scoreboard isn't in their favor.

THE DANGER OF "TOXIC POSITIVITY"

It is worth noting that positivity without truth is dangerous. I have seen leaders try to motivate by ignoring real issues. It does not inspire; it frustrates. True leadership optimism rests on three qualities. First, honesty: acknowledging reality clearly. Second, belief: demonstrating confidence that the team can improve. Third, action: presenting a path forward that everyone can work on. Without these, positivity becomes hollow cheerleading, and people eventually tune out.

A CORPORATE STORY

In one of my corporate leadership roles, our region missed its targets for cadence calls and diversity of engagement for three consecutive months. The pressure from above was intense, and there were potential consequences, including staffing changes and some associates possibly having to exit the business. I could have called a meeting and said, "We need to hit our numbers, no excuses."

Instead, I acknowledged the reality: "We are not where we need to be. I know that, and you know that. But I believe we have the talent to get there, and here is the plan we are going to execute together."

We broke the goal into smaller weekly milestones, celebrated small wins along the way, and adjusted the plan when needed. Within two months, we were back on track.

When I first introduced the new plan, the room was quiet. You could feel the skepticism. A few team members had that "Here we go again" look; we'd tried big turnaround plans before, and none of them stuck. One person even asked, "How is this any different from the last one?"

I didn't try to sell them with hype. Instead, I said, "This isn't about fixing everything overnight. It's about improving 1% each week, one metric, one behavior, one client experience at a time." That reframing shifted the tone. The goal suddenly felt achievable, not overwhelming.

My strategy going in was simple: break the big target into weekly milestones, celebrate every win (no matter how small), and make adjustments together. The first few weeks were all about consistency, short, focused check-ins, open communication, and visible recognition when someone moved the needle, even slightly.

By week three, the mood had changed. People were smiling in meetings, sharing ideas instead of just status updates. Confidence started to replace burnout. Within two months, we weren't just back on track, we were outperforming our original projections.

Looking back, I realize I was already thinking in terms of the 1% Push even before I had the name for it. It wasn't a strategy on paper; it was a mindset in action: small shifts, big wins, lasting leadership.

Positivity wasn't about pretending everything was fine. It was about making the team believe improvement was possible and then showing them how to get there.

FRAMEWORK: THE ACE METHOD FOR POSITIVE LEADERSHIP

1. **A – Acknowledge Reality:** Be transparent about where things stand. Sugarcoating destroys credibility.
2. **C – Create Belief:** Share your confidence in the team's ability to improve and why you believe it's possible.
3. **E – Establish the Path Forward:** Lay out the next steps clearly so optimism is tied to action.

THE LINK BETWEEN POSITIVITY AND ACCOUNTABILITY

Here's an important truth: *positivity without accountability is useless.*

If you only encourage but never challenge, your team will feel supported but stagnant. If you only challenge without encouragement, they'll feel pushed but drained. The magic is in the balance, showing belief in people while also expecting their best.

The key to balancing positivity and accountability is knowing your people and pacing your pressure. You earn the right to challenge someone by first showing that you understand them. Every person responds differently; some need direct feedback to rise, while others need confidence before correction.

My method is simple: Lead with belief, follow with truth, and finish with support.

1. **Lead with Belief:** Start by affirming what's working, recognizing effort, attitude, or progress. This establishes trust and opens the door for growth.
2. "I know you've been giving your all on this project..."
3. **Follow with Truth:** Be specific and honest about where improvement is needed. Accountability without clarity is just pressure.
4. "...but we've missed a few key deadlines. Let's talk about what's getting in the way."
5. **Finish with Support:** End by reinforcing partnership, not punishment.
6. "I believe you can get this back on track. What can I do to help remove obstacles?"

That sequence keeps accountability human. You're not avoiding tough conversations; you're framing them with belief. The result is growth without resentment, drive without burnout.

In other words, empathy opens the door, accountability raises the standard, and balance keeps people walking through it.

A great coach doesn't just say, "I believe in you." They say, "I believe in you, and I expect you to run this play with everything you've got, because I know you can do it."

> **LOCKER ROOM LESSON**
> *Positivity isn't about ignoring the score.*
> *It's about believing the score can change.*

REFLECTION QUESTIONS

1. How do you currently respond when your team faces setbacks?
2. Are you balancing encouragement with accountability?
3. When was the last time you reframed a problem into an opportunity for your team?

ACTION STEPS

- In your next meeting, start by acknowledging a challenge; then share why you believe your team can overcome it.
- Identify one person on your team who needs encouragement right now. Give them a specific, genuine piece of feedback this week.
- Practice reframing: the next time a challenge arises, present it with "Here's how we can win this" language.

REAL LIFE STORY: THE LOCKER ROOM BEFORE THE STORM

It was the semifinal playoff game. The stakes were high, and so was the tension. We'd just finished the first half, and it wasn't pretty. We were down by fifteen points, the crowd was restless, and the energy in the locker room was heavy.

I've been in rooms like that before, and I've seen two possible outcomes:

1. The negativity spreads like wildfire, pulling the team even lower.
2. Someone chooses to change the temperature in the room.

That night, it was our team captain. He didn't give a fiery speech, and he didn't sugarcoat the situation. He simply walked in, smiled, and said, "Well... the good news is, we only need to win one half of basketball. And last time I checked, we're pretty good at that."

Everyone laughed. Shoulders dropped. The tension broke. And you could feel the shift, not just in mood, but in belief. We went back out, played loose, and ended up winning by six points.

THE LEADERSHIP LESSON

Positivity isn't about ignoring problems; it's about refusing to let the problem define the outcome. When leaders set a tone of optimism, it changes how teams respond under pressure.

In business, markets shift, budgets tighten, and challenges come fast. A leader's ability to anchor the team in possibility instead of fear becomes a competitive advantage. People perform better when they believe a win is still possible.

A positive mindset won't guarantee victory,
but a negative one will guarantee defeat.

TAKEAWAY FOR LEADERS

The real competitive advantage isn't just strategy or skill, it's mindset. And mindset is contagious. As a leader, your tone in tough moments becomes the ceiling or the springboard for your team's performance.

Key Takeaway: Positivity is not about blind optimism. It's about honest belief in your team's ability to improve and the willingness to lead them there. Done right, it becomes one of the most powerful competitive advantages you can have as a leader.

CHAPTER 5
CREATING YOUR LEADERSHIP PLAYBOOK

When I played professional basketball, every team I was part of had a playbook. It wasn't just a stack of plays on paper; it was our identity.

The playbook defined how we played, why we played that way, and what we'd do in different situations. It gave us structure, consistency, and confidence.

Without it, we'd just show up and wing it. Relying on individual talent and hoping for the best. And here's the truth: that's exactly how too many leaders operate in business.

They step into leadership roles without a clear philosophy or framework and then wonder why their teams lack consistency and cohesion. If you want sustained success as a leader, you need your own leadership playbook.

WHY YOU NEED A PLAYBOOK AS A LEADER

A playbook in leadership does three things:

1. **Clarifies your philosophy** – Your team knows what you stand for and how you make decisions.
2. **Creates alignment** – Everyone understands the "rules of the game" and the non-negotiables.
3. **Builds consistency** – You lead with the same principles whether you're under pressure or in a win streak.

Without a playbook, leadership becomes reactive. With one, it becomes intentional.

A LESSON FROM THE SIDELINES

I remember joining a team halfway through the season. They had talented players, but no identity. One night, they played fast; the next, they slowed it down. Some players hustled on defense; others barely moved.

Our coach came in and did something radical: before changing a single play, he brought us into a room and said, "First, we decide who we are."

We talked for hours about our strengths, weaknesses, and what kind of team we wanted to be. Then we built our playbook to reflect that. Within weeks, we went from unpredictable and inconsistent to a team that knew exactly how we wanted to win.

Leaders in business need to do the same. They decide who they are and build a playbook that makes it real.

THE 1% PUSH IN YOUR PLAYBOOK

Your playbook doesn't have to be fifty pages long. It's about small, repeatable habits that shape culture and performance:

- How you open and close meetings
- The way you give feedback
- The expectations you set for communication

- The way you recognize and celebrate wins

These things may seem minor, but they send constant signals to your team about what matters, and over time, they create a distinct leadership identity.

BUILDING BLOCKS OF A LEADERSHIP PLAYBOOK

Here's how I recommend building your own playbook, step-by-step:

1. Define Your Leadership Philosophy

Ask yourself:

- *What do I believe about leadership?*
- *What do I expect from my team?*
- *What can they expect from me?*

Write these down in a short, clear statement.

Example: "I believe leadership is about empowering others to succeed while holding them accountable to their highest potential."

2. Identify Your Non-Negotiables

These are the things you will never compromise on: your version of "team rules."

- Always tell the truth.
- Communicate with respect.
- Follow through on commitments.

3. Map Your Key Plays

In basketball, a "play" is a planned approach to a specific situation. In leadership, your plays are the strategies you use for:

- Onboarding new team members.
- Handling performance issues.
- Running effective meetings.
- Responding to crises.

Document how you approach each so you can execute consistently.

4. Create Your Feedback Philosophy

Feedback is one of the most defining elements of a leader's playbook. Decide:

- How often will you give feedback?
- Will it be public or private?
- How will you balance positive and corrective feedback?

5. Design Your Recognition System

Recognition is not random in a great culture; it's built into the game plan. Decide:

- What behaviors will you recognize?
- How will you celebrate wins (big and small)?

A CORPORATE STORY

When I stepped into a leadership role at my Fortune 500 company, I realized my team had no consistent approach to client engagement.

Each person had their own style, which created uneven results. So we built a Client Engagement Playbook together:

- Every client received a monthly touchpoint.
- Every conversation included a value-based question.
- Every unresolved client issue was escalated within forty-eight hours.

It wasn't complicated, but because it was consistent, results improved quickly. Clients felt a stronger connection, and the team felt more confident because they knew exactly what was expected.

THE DANGER OF NO PLAYBOOK

Without a playbook, you're left with inconsistent execution (some team members deliver excellence while others don't), confusion (people aren't sure what "good" looks like), and leader burnout (your time is spent solving problems that clearer expectations could have prevented). In sports, no playbook means chaos on the court; in business, it means chaos in your culture.

FRAMEWORK: THE 5P LEADERSHIP PLAYBOOK MODEL

P1 – **Philosophy:** Your core beliefs about leadership.
P2 – **Principles:** Your non-negotiable rules and values.
P3 – **Plays:** Your repeatable strategies for common situations.
P4 – **People Development:** How you grow and empower talent.
P5 – **Performance Management:** How you measure and maintain standards

THE 1% PUSH APPLICATION

You don't have to create your playbook all at once. Start with one section, such as your feedback philosophy, and commit to applying it consistently. Once that's solid, move to the next.

Just like in sports, you don't memorize the whole playbook in one practice; you learn it piece by piece, applying it until it becomes second nature.

> **LOCKER ROOM LESSON**
> *Talent wins games, but a clear playbook wins seasons.*

REFLECTION QUESTIONS

1. If your team had to describe your leadership style in three words, what would they say?
2. What are your non-negotiables as a leader?
3. Which area of your leadership most needs a clear, repeatable "play" right now?

ACTION STEPS

- Write your leadership philosophy in one to two sentences this week.
- Identify three non-negotiables and communicate them to your team.
- Document one "play" for a recurring leadership situation you face.

REAL LIFE STORY: THE SEASON WE STARTED FROM SCRATCH

One year, my basketball team went through a massive roster change. We lost half our starters, brought in young players, and switched to a new head coach.

At our first team meeting, everyone expected the coach to walk in with a massive binder of plays, rules, and strategies. Instead, he brought a blank notebook.

He said, "We're not here to copy last season's playbook. We're going to build one that works for us, with the people we have, and the way we want to play."

Over the next several weeks, we built that playbook together. We experimented in practice, tried new rotations, learned each other's strengths and weaknesses, and slowly defined our identity as a team. The result wasn't just a set of plays; it was a shared understanding of how we operated, what we valued, and how we responded to challenges.

By the time the playoffs came, we didn't have to flip through pages to know what to do. Our playbook lived in our heads and in our trust for one another.

THE LEADERSHIP LESSON

Too many leaders try to copy someone else's "proven" playbook without adapting it to their team, culture, or current reality. But a playbook isn't just a set of instructions; it's a living, breathing framework built from shared experiences, team input, and real-world challenges.

The best playbook isn't borrowed, it's built.

TAKEAWAY FOR LEADERS

Your leadership playbook should be personal, practical, and adaptable. It should reflect not just what you want to achieve, but how you and your team are going to achieve it together, a single 1% Push at a time.

———

Key Takeaway: Great leadership is not improvised; it's intentional. Build your playbook, and you'll give your team the clarity, consistency, and confidence they need to win.

CHAPTER 6
THE ART OF THE 1% PUSH IN DAILY LEADERSHIP

When people hear "The 1% Push," they often think it's about doing more work. It's not. It's about doing the right, little things consistently that lead to outsized results over time.

In sports, a 1% improvement might be running one more sprint, watching a few extra minutes of game film, or perfecting a single movement in your shot. In leadership, it's about the micro-actions, the small pushes, that compound into major wins.

The 1% Push is where the mindset of empowering leadership meets the discipline of execution.

WHY SMALL PUSHES MATTER?

Let's do the math.
After one day, you're at:
$1.01^1 = 1.01 \rightarrow 1\%$ better
After 2 days:
$1.01^2 = 1.0201 \rightarrow 2.01\%$ better
...and so on.

After 365 days (one year), you've improved:

$1.01^{365} = 37.78\%$

If you improve by 1% every day for a year, you'll be more than thirty-seven times better than you were at the start, or 3,778% better! That's the power of compounding in action.

Now, the reverse is also true. If you let yourself get 1% worse each day, a little less effort, a little more complacency, you'll find yourself in a massive performance hole before you even realize it.

In leadership, the gap between those two trajectories is the difference between a high-performing, engaged team and one that's stagnant or disengaged.

A GAME-WINNING EXAMPLE

I once played for a coach who had a "1% Rule." After every practice, we had to spend five minutes improving one skill: a free throw, a defensive slide, or a passing drill. Five minutes doesn't sound like much, but over the course of the season, it made a massive difference.

I remember one season where free throws were our "Achilles' heel." In the first month, we were shooting barely 62% from the line, and it was costing us close games. We'd play great for thirty-nine minutes, only to lose by a point or two because of missed opportunities at the stripe.

That's when our coach introduced the 1% Rule. After every practice, we spent just five extra minutes shooting free throws, no fancy drills, no pressure, just quiet repetition and focus. Everyone tracked their makes individually, and we posted the team average on the locker room board each week. Also, everybody needed to make five in a row before going to the locker room.

At first, it didn't seem to change much. But by midseason, something shifted, and players started trusting their routine. The numbers climbed from 62% to 72% and then to 78% by the end of the season.

It all came together in an important game at the end of the season. Down by one with seconds left, our center, who'd been a 55%

shooter at the start of the year, got fouled. He hit both shots, and we won by a single point.

That season taught me what five minutes a day can do. The extra reps didn't just improve our technique; they built confidence. And when the pressure was highest, that consistency turned into calm.

That's the power of the 1% Push: a small, steady effort that compounds into big results when it matters most.

That rule didn't just make us better players; it made us think like professionals. We started asking ourselves daily, *What's my 1% today?*

Imagine if every leader asked themselves that same question about their team: What's my 1% Push for them today?

THE 1% PUSH LEADERSHIP MINDSET

The beauty of the 1% Push is that it removes the pressure of massive, overnight transformation; instead, it focuses on intentionality, consistency, and relevance, ensuring each day includes at least one act aimed at growth, applying the practice regularly enough to build momentum, and tailoring each push to the person or situation.

DAILY 1% PUSH OPPORTUNITIES

Here's where leaders often miss the mark. They think pushes have to be grand. In reality, the most impactful ones are small, specific, and personal.

Examples:

- Giving a team member a stretch assignment slightly outside their comfort zone:

I once asked an associate to co-lead a client presentation, something she'd never done before. She was nervous, but I paired her with a mentor and checked in during prep. She nailed it, and that experience unlocked a new level of confidence.

- Offering targeted feedback immediately after observing a behavior:

After a meeting, I pulled a team member aside and said, "Your insights were strong, but your delivery was rushed. Take a breath before each point next time." The feedback was specific, timely, and actionable. In the next meeting, his presence completely changed.

- Recognizing effort in real time, not just results at the end of the quarter:

During a tough week, I noticed one rep staying late to help others troubleshoot client issues. I called it out in our morning huddle the next day. That thirty-second recognition boosted not just his morale, but the entire team's energy.

- Asking a thought-provoking question in a one-on-one instead of giving direct instructions.

Instead of telling a team member how to handle a challenging client, I asked, "If you were the client, what would build your trust right now?" That question shifted his mindset from reaction to empathy, and he came up with a better solution than I would have.

Each of these moments is a 1% Push, small, intentional leadership choices that build confidence, accountability, and ownership one person at a time.

THE THREE TYPES OF 1% PUSHES

1. **Skill Push** – Improving technical or professional ability

Example: "Let's work on how you open client calls to set a stronger tone."

2. **Mindset Push** – Encouraging a shift in perspective

Example: "Instead of thinking about why this won't work, what's one way it could?"

3. **Ownership Push** – Building independence and leadership in others

Example: "You lead the next project update. I'll be there to support, but you run the room."

A CORPORATE STORY

When I was mentoring a promising young leader in my corporate role, I noticed she tended to avoid conflict. When team members missed deadlines or underperformed, she'd quietly fix the issue herself instead of addressing it. It kept the peace in the short term, but created bigger problems later. Her team started assuming she'd always step in.

I gave her a 1% Push: "Next time an issue comes up, address it within twenty-four hours. Even if it's uncomfortable, just start the conversation."

Her first attempt was rough. She confronted a team member about missed deliverables, but her voice shook and the message came out softer than intended. Still, she did it, and that was the win. Afterward, we talked through what worked, what didn't, and how to use facts and curiosity instead of frustration.

Each week, she got a little better, asking clear questions, setting expectations, and following up consistently. Within two months, she wasn't just having the tough conversations; she was leading them with confidence.

The change was noticeable. Accountability improved, results followed, and her team started viewing her not just as approachable but as a leader they respected. One small "push" toward discomfort had a massive ripple effect for her, her team, and the culture around her.

FRAMEWORK: THE PUSH MODEL

- **P – Pinpoint the Opportunity:** Identify a specific area where growth is possible.
- **U – Understand the Person:** Know their strengths, challenges, and what motivates them.
- **S – Shape the Push:** Design a small, actionable step they can take now.
- **H – Hold Them Accountable:** Follow up and reinforce the change until it sticks.

BALANCING PUSH AND SUPPORT

A push without support feels like pressure. Support without a push feels like comfort.

Your job as a leader is to balance both: push (challenging people to go beyond their current limits) and support (providing the tools, coaching, and encouragement they need to succeed). Think of it like a strength coach spotting an athlete: the athlete lifts the weight, but the coach is right there if help is needed.

THE 1% PUSH FOR YOURSELF

This isn't just about your team; it's about you, too. If you're not pushing yourself by even 1% each day, you're asking your team to do something you're not modeling. That might mean learning one new skill each week, seeking feedback from a peer or mentor, or spending ten minutes a day reading about leadership trends. When your team sees you growing, they're far more likely to grow themselves.

A few years ago, I challenged myself to model the 1% Push. Each week, I focused on one small improvement. One week, it was learning a new presentation skill, and another week, it was asking a peer for honest feedback on how I showed up in meetings. I also committed to reading ten minutes a day on leadership and mindset.

At first, it felt small, almost insignificant, but within weeks, my energy and perspective shifted. I started sharing what I was learning in team meetings, and soon others followed. One teammate began doing short, daily reflections; another started reading with me.

Those micro-habits caught on because growth is contagious. When your team sees you stretching, even slightly, they realize improvement isn't about perfection—it's about progress. That's the 1% Push in action.

SPORTS ANALOGY: CHAMPIONSHIP TEAMS ARE BUILT ON 1% PUSHES

A powerful example comes from the 2001 New England Patriots season. They did not dominate from day one, and they certainly did not look like a championship team early on. After losing their franchise quarterback and starting the year with low expectations, the Patriots leaned into constant micro-adjustments: refining play-calling, adapting matchups week by week, improving conditioning, and building system discipline around a young and unproven Tom Brady. Those incremental shifts compounded over the season, and by the time they reached the Super Bowl, they were a completely different team, proving that championships are built through consistent, small improvements rather than single-moment breakthroughs.

In leadership, those micro-adjustments are your 1% Push. Over time, they transform your culture, your team's capability, and your results.

> **LOCKER ROOM LESSON**
> *Small pushes create big wins, but only if you give them every day.*

REFLECTION QUESTIONS

1. Who on your team needs a skill push right now?
2. Who could benefit from a mindset shift?
3. Where do you need to give yourself a 1% Push?

ACTION STEPS

- Identify three people on your team. Decide whether they need a skill, mindset, or ownership push this week.
- Deliver the push, then follow up within a week to reinforce it.
- Commit to one personal 1% Push for the next thirty days.

REAL LIFE STORY: THE POWER OF SMALL WINS

When I first took over a new corporate team, I walked into a situation where morale was low, performance was inconsistent, and deadlines felt like moving targets. The temptation was to overhaul everything at once: new systems, new goals, new metrics.

But I knew that a sudden, massive change would overwhelm people. Instead, I started introducing the 1% Push.

I asked each team member to pick one small, achievable improvement they could focus on every day for the next month, something that wouldn't disrupt their whole workflow but would steadily raise their game. For one person, it was making proactive client calls before issues came up. For another, it was sending follow-up notes within twenty-four hours instead of waiting until the end of the week.

At first, it didn't feel like much. But after a few weeks, we began to see a shift, not just in numbers, but in confidence. Small wins stacked into bigger ones. The team started hitting targets early. And more importantly, they started believing they could keep improving.

The Leadership Lesson

The 1% Push is not about giant leaps; it's about deliberate, consistent nudges that compound over time. When leaders help their people focus on daily, manageable growth, it removes the fear of failure and replaces it with momentum.

Big wins are built one small push at a time.

TAKEAWAY FOR LEADERS

You don't have to transform your team in a day. You just have to move them forward by 1% every single day. Over time, those small pushes don't just improve performance; they redefine what your people believe is possible.

Key Takeaway: Leadership excellence doesn't come from grand gestures; it comes from the small, intentional pushes you give your team every day. Those 1% improvements, stacked over time, are how you build lasting success.

CHAPTER 7
ACCOUNTABILITY WITHOUT FEAR

When most people hear "accountability," they immediately think of punishment: a negative meeting, a stern email, or someone "being called out." But in great teams, whether on the court or in the office, accountability isn't a threat; it's a sign of respect. It means you believe in someone enough to hold them to a higher standard.

In fact, one of the highest compliments you can give a teammate is to hold them accountable, because it means you care about their success and the success of the team.

WHY ACCOUNTABILITY HAS A BAD REPUTATION

The reason so many leaders avoid holding people accountable is that they've seen it done badly. They've seen leaders:

- Wait too long to address an issue, so frustration builds and the conversation explodes.
- Focus on blame instead of solutions.

- Make accountability personal rather than performance-based.

When accountability is delivered with judgment, it creates fear. When it is delivered with care, it creates growth.

SPORTS ANALOGY: CHAMPIONSHIP TEAMS DEMAND ACCOUNTABILITY

In my pro basketball career, the best teams I played for weren't afraid of accountability; they expected it.

We had a simple rule: you could make a mistake, but you couldn't make the same mistake twice without hearing about it. And it didn't matter if you were a rookie or a veteran; if you missed a defensive assignment, a teammate would let you know.

That rule made us better because it created collective accountability. It wasn't about blame, it was about belief. When someone called you out, it wasn't personal; it meant they trusted you to do better. The message was: "You're too good to keep making the same mistake."

It built a culture where feedback flowed in every direction, rookie to veteran, starter to bench player. We stopped taking corrections as criticism and started seeing it as commitment. That constant awareness tightened our defense, sharpened our focus, and made us play for each other, not just with each other.

In short, that rule turned accountability into respect, and that's what transformed us from a group of players into a real team.

The key? It was never about you as a person. It was about what you did and how it affected the team. That distinction made all the difference.

THE LINK BETWEEN ACCOUNTABILITY AND THE 1% PUSH

Accountability is the natural partner of the 1% Push.

- The 1% Push says, "I believe you can grow."
- Accountability says, "I am going to make sure you do."

Without accountability, a push is just encouragement. Without a push, accountability feels like criticism. Together, they drive real improvement.

Here is the shift leaders need to make: accountability is not done to someone; it is done with them.

- Instead of: "You are not meeting expectations."
- Try: "I know you are capable of more, and I want to help you get there."

This approach turns accountability from a punishment into a partnership.

A CORPORATE STORY

A few years ago, I worked with a manager who dreaded performance conversations. She would sugarcoat everything to avoid making people uncomfortable.

The result? Her team's performance lagged because no one knew how far off they were from expectations.

We worked together to shift her approach using the CARE Method:

- Clarify expectations early and often.
- Assess performance honestly.
- Respectfully deliver the feedback.

- Equip the person with tools or next steps to improve.

Within three months, her team's numbers improved, not because she became "tougher," but because she became clearer and more consistent.

THE THREE RULES OF FEARLESS ACCOUNTABILITY

1. **Address Issues Early** – Problems don't get smaller with time.
2. **Focus on the Behavior, Not the Person** – Separate identity from action.
3. **End with a Path Forward** – Accountability without a solution is just criticism.

SPORTS ANALOGY: THE FILM ROOM

One of the toughest but most effective accountability tools in sports is the film room. After a game, we'd watch footage of our plays: the good, the bad, and the ugly.

When you saw your missed rotation on the screen, there was no hiding. But here's the thing, the film session wasn't about embarrassment. It was about learning what to do differently next time.

Business leaders can create their own "film room" moments by reviewing projects, presentations, or client calls in a constructive way. The goal is improvement, not humiliation.

FRAMEWORK: THE 4A MODEL FOR ACCOUNTABILITY

A1 – Align Expectations: Start by making sure everyone knows what success looks like.
A2 – Assess the Gap: Identify the difference between current performance and the goal.
A3 – Act with Empathy: Deliver feedback in a way that preserves dignity and trust.
A4 – Agree on Next Steps: Collaboratively define what will change and how you'll measure it.

THE ROLE OF TRUST IN ACCOUNTABILITY

Remember from Chapter 3: Trust gets you in the door; value keeps you in the room.

Accountability works best when trust is already in place. When people believe you have their best interests at heart, they're far more likely to receive accountability as a gift rather than a threat.

THE 1% PUSH APPLICATION

Use accountability to deliver small, consistent pushes instead of big, intimidating interventions. For example, instead of waiting for a quarterly review, address a small issue in real time; instead of letting frustration build, ask a clarifying question in the moment, such as "What happened there, and what will you do differently next time?" These micro-corrections keep performance aligned without damaging morale.

> **LOCKER ROOM LESSON**
> *Accountability isn't about calling someone out;*
> *it's about calling them up.*

REFLECTION QUESTIONS

1. How do you currently approach accountability, with fear or with partnership?
2. Are you addressing performance issues early enough?
3. Do your team members know you hold them accountable because you believe in them?

ACTION STEPS

- This week, identify one performance gap and address it directly using the CARE Method.
- Review your last three accountability conversations. Did they end with a clear path forward?
- Ask a trusted peer to hold you accountable for one leadership habit you want to improve.

REAL LIFE STORY: THE SEASON THAT WASN'T SUPPOSED TO HAPPEN

In one of my basketball seasons, we weren't expected to go far. The roster was young, the preseason rankings had us near the bottom, and honestly, even some of the fans were just hoping we'd have a "respectable" year.

Instead of obsessing over the championship, our coach set a single goal: to win the next practice. Not the next game, the next practice. He challenged us to find just one thing we could improve on every day.

Some days, that meant shaving two seconds off a fast break drill. Other days, it meant increasing free-throw percentages by a single point. They were small wins, almost invisible on their own, but they stacked like bricks.

By mid-season, we were no longer playing catch-up. We were dictating the pace. By playoff time, we weren't the underdogs anymore; we were the team nobody wanted to face. And when the final buzzer sounded on the championship game, we were holding the trophy that "wasn't supposed" to be ours.

THE LEADERSHIP LESSON

Big wins rarely come from giant leaps. They come from the discipline of showing up, making one intentional improvement each day, and letting those improvements compound.

In leadership, the same applies. You build culture, trust, and performance brick by brick. The 1% Push isn't about intensity; it's about consistency.

Championships aren't won in one game; they're earned in a thousand tiny moments nobody sees.

TAKEAWAY FOR LEADERS

You don't need a miracle to create a breakthrough. You just need to keep stacking the small wins until the scoreboard tells a very different story.

Key Takeaway: Accountability without fear is one of the most powerful leadership tools you can use. It creates clarity, drives performance, and builds trust, especially when paired with the 1% Push philosophy.

CHAPTER 8
EMPOWERMENT IN ACTION

In leadership, empowerment isn't about letting go completely; it's about giving people the freedom to act with confidence while knowing you've set them up to succeed.

In sports, no coach wins by micromanaging every move during the game. They win by preparing their team so well in practice that, once the whistle blows, the players can adapt, think, and execute on their own.

The same principle applies in business. Your team's true performance is measured when you're not in the room.

WHY EMPOWERMENT MATTERS

Empowerment creates three powerful outcomes:

1. **Ownership** – People take responsibility for results because they feel trusted.
2. **Confidence** – They believe they have the skills and authority to make decisions.

3. **Innovation** – They're more likely to try new approaches without fear of punishment.

SPORTS ANALOGY: THE POINT GUARD'S FREEDOM

As a pro basketball player, I learned that the most empowered position on the court was the point guard. The coach gave them the playbook, the strategy, and the trust to run the offense in real time.

Sure, the coach could call a timeout to make adjustments, but during the flow of the game, the point guard made dozens of decisions without asking for permission. That's empowerment: preparation plus trust.

I remember one coach who worked closely with our point guard after every practice. Instead of overloading him with plays, he'd focus on one scenario, reading a double team, adjusting tempo, or communicating better on fast breaks. Each day, one small improvement.

Over time, those 1% pushes added up. By midseason, our point guard wasn't looking to the bench for direction anymore; he was anticipating defenses, leading huddles, and controlling the game's rhythm. The coach didn't just build a player; he built a leader, one decision at a time.

THE 1% PUSH IN EMPOWERMENT

Empowerment doesn't mean giving someone the keys and hoping they figure it out. It's about giving them progressive responsibility, starting small and increasing freedom as they prove they can handle it.

A 1% Push in empowerment could be:

- Letting someone lead part of a meeting instead of the whole thing.
- Giving them a small budget to manage before handling a larger one.
- Asking them to propose solutions instead of just problems.

These incremental steps build capability without overwhelming them.

A CORPORATE STORY

I once led a team where one member was incredibly talented but hesitant to make decisions. She'd always come to me for approval, even on small matters.

I gave her a 1% Push: "For the next two weeks, you don't need my sign-off on anything under $500. I trust you to decide."

At first, she was nervous. But within a month, she was making faster, smarter decisions, and her confidence skyrocketed. Eventually, she was leading major projects without hesitation.

FRAMEWORK: THE EARN MODEL FOR EMPOWERMENT

- **E – Establish Clear Boundaries:** People can't operate confidently if they don't know the limits. Define what's in their control.
- **A – Align on the Goal:** Make sure they understand the bigger picture and desired outcome.
- **R – Resource Them:** Give them the tools, information, and support they need to succeed.

- **N – Nurture Growth:** Provide feedback, celebrate wins, and help them expand their range of responsibility over time.

BALANCING EMPOWERMENT AND ACCOUNTABILITY

Empowerment does not mean less accountability. The two go hand in hand.

Empowerment without accountability leads to chaos. Accountability without empowerment leads to frustration. The sweet spot is giving people the autonomy to act while holding them to the agreed-upon standards.

I once led a project where I gave the team complete freedom to design a new client process, no checkpoints, no timelines. I wanted to show trust, but without clear accountability, direction drifted, and deadlines slipped.

The next project, I overcorrected, with tight controls, daily check-ins, and every detail reviewed. The team hit the deadlines but lost energy and ownership.

It was the third attempt that proved the model: clear goals, regular but brief check-ins, and full decision-making power within their roles. The team felt trusted and responsible, and the results spoke for themselves.

Think of it like coaching a team. You let them play the game, but you still review the performance and make adjustments.

THE TRUST EQUATION

Empowerment works only when trust flows both ways. The leader must trust the team to make decisions and act responsibly, and the team must trust the leader to have their back if mistakes happen. Without this mutual trust, empowerment feels risky instead of motivating.

Here is a sports analogy: the play-calling test. Some coaches I had would stop calling plays entirely for a quarter during practice, and the team had to figure out the offense on its own. The first few possessions were often messy, but over time, we learned to read the defense, communicate on the fly, and make smart decisions.

Business leaders can apply the same idea by giving the team space to solve a problem without jumping in right away.

THE 1% PUSH FOR YOURSELF AS A LEADER

Empowerment is also a discipline for the leader. It means resisting the urge to jump in and "fix" everything. Your personal 1% Push could be holding back from giving the answer immediately and instead asking, "What do you think we should do?" delegating one more decision each week than you normally would, and giving someone full ownership of a small project from start to finish.

Common empowerment pitfalls:

1. **No clarity:** People cannot be empowered if they do not know what success looks like.
2. **Overload:** Giving too much responsibility too soon without the skills or resources to handle it.
3. **Taking it back:** Assigning responsibility but jumping in to control the outcome the moment it gets tough.

> **LOCKER ROOM LESSON**
> *Empowerment isn't stepping back; it's stepping aside so others can step up.*

REFLECTION QUESTIONS

1. Where are you currently holding onto control that you could hand over?
2. Who on your team is ready for a 1% Push in empowerment?
3. How clear are your boundaries and expectations for empowered decisions?

ACTION STEPS

- Identify one task or decision you can delegate this week with clear boundaries and a defined outcome.
- Schedule a check-in to provide feedback and guidance without taking control back.
- Celebrate the effort and learning as much as the result.

REAL LIFE STORY: THE GAME I DIDN'T PLAY

During my basketball career, there was a playoff game where I barely touched the ball, not because I wasn't ready to play, but because my job that night was different. I'd been mentoring a younger teammate all season, pushing him in practice, giving him small challenges to build his confidence.

When the big night came, our coach looked at me and said, "Tonight, it's his game. You've already done your part; now, let him take the shot."

And he did. Again and again. He hit career highs in points and rebounds that night, and we won.

Walking off the court, a reporter asked if I was frustrated about not scoring much. I just smiled and said, "I didn't need to score tonight. I already made my impact."

THE LEADERSHIP LESSON

Empowerment means knowing when to step back so others can step forward. It's not about giving people tasks; it's about giving them ownership.

When you've invested time coaching, guiding, and trusting someone, their win becomes your win. And over time, the team learns that success isn't measured by individual stats; it's measured by how much we lift each other.

> *A leader's greatest victory is watching someone they coached win the game.*

TAKEAWAY FOR LEADERS

Empowerment in action means building people's capability and confidence so that when the moment comes, they don't just execute; they excel. Sometimes the best leadership move isn't taking the shot yourself, but creating the conditions for someone else to make it.

Key Takeaway: Empowerment in action means preparing people, trusting them to act, and supporting their growth, while maintaining the accountability that keeps performance high. Done right, it's one of the most powerful 1% pushes you can give.

CHAPTER 9
THE RIPPLE EFFECT OF THE 1% PUSH

When you drop a pebble into a still pond, the ripples spread far beyond the point of impact. That's what leadership is like. Every decision you make, every conversation you have, every push you give, doesn't just affect the moment; it shapes the future.

The challenge is that most leaders underestimate how far those ripples travel. The 1% Push is powerful not because of its size, but because of its consistency. A single conversation can spark a change in mindset, a boost in confidence, or a shift in behavior, and when that person interacts with others, they carry that change forward.

Over time, small pushes compound into:

- **Cultural shifts** – A team moves from reactive to proactive.
- **Performance improvements** – Metrics trend upward because habits have changed.
- **Talent development** – People grow into leaders themselves.

THE ASSIST THAT WINS THE GAME

In basketball, there's a stat that often gets overlooked: the assist. An assist doesn't score points directly, but without it, the basket wouldn't happen.

A 1% Push is like an assist. You may not always see the final result, but you've set it in motion. And just like in sports, the more assists you give, the stronger your team becomes.

A CORPORATE STORY

Several years ago, I worked with a young sales rep who was talented but inconsistent. In one coaching session, I gave her a 1% Push: "Before every client call, write down the single most valuable outcome you want for the customer."

She started doing it religiously. Her calls became more focused, her clients felt more heard, and her close rate improved. But here's the ripple effect: she taught the habit to her peers. Within months, the entire team was using it, and the team's numbers across the board jumped.

That's the ripple effect, one push, many waves.

THE CULTURAL RIPPLE

When leaders consistently give 1% pushes, they create a culture where growth, feedback, and accountability are normal. This culture then sustains itself, even when the leader isn't directly involved.

- A culture of feedback leads to self-correcting teams.

When feedback becomes part of the daily rhythm, teams stop waiting for annual reviews to improve. They coach each other in real time, fix small issues before they grow, and build mutual trust through honesty. It's the ultimate expression of the 1% Push: small adjustments, made consistently, that compound into continuous improvement.

- A culture of recognition leads to higher engagement.

When leaders celebrate effort as much as outcomes, people feel seen. Recognition fuels motivation, strengthens belonging, and reinforces the behaviors that drive results. A simple "I noticed what you did there" can shift someone's day or their career. In the 1% Push, every acknowledgment becomes a spark that keeps the fire of performance burning.

- A culture of ownership leads to faster decision-making.

When people trust themselves to act and know they're trusted by their leaders, they stop waiting for permission and start driving results. Ownership turns accountability into pride. It empowers teams to think, decide, and adapt faster because when everyone takes responsibility for progress, momentum becomes unstoppable.

THE LONG GAME

The true ripple effect of leadership often can't be measured in days or even months. Sometimes, the seeds you plant now don't fully grow until years later.

I've had former team members reach out years after we worked together to tell me that a single piece of advice or a challenge I gave them changed the trajectory of their career. At the time, I had no idea it had that impact. I was just doing my job.

It was something I barely remembered saying. After a tough quarter, she was discouraged and ready to play it safe. I told her, "You don't grow by staying comfortable. Take one step that scares you and prove to yourself you can handle it."

She later told me that a single line pushed her to apply for a leadership role she didn't think she was ready for. She got the job, and years later, she's still growing from that moment.

That's when it hit me: as leaders, the words that feel small to us can be life-changing to someone else. A simple 1% Push, the right challenge at the right time, can alter someone's entire path.

This is why the 1% Push matters so much; you never know which small moment will be the one that sticks.

FRAMEWORK: THE RIPPLE MODEL

- R – Recognize small moments where you can make a difference.
- I – Initiate action instead of waiting for the perfect time.
- P – Personalize the push to the individual.
- P – Provide support and resources.
- L – Lead by example so others follow.
- E – Expand the habit by encouraging people to pay it forward.

SPORTS ANALOGY: PASSING IT ON

In every great sports program, veteran players mentor the rookies. They pass on not just skills, but culture: how to prepare, how to handle pressure, how to win and lose with class.

In leadership, your goal is to create "veterans" who will carry your philosophy forward long after you've moved on. That's the ultimate ripple effect.

THE 1% PUSH AS A LEGACY

When you give a 1% Push, you're not just improving performance today; you're building a legacy of growth and leadership. Your pushes may inspire someone to take on a leadership role, equip a team to handle challenges more effectively, and influence how they lead their own teams in the future.

A RIPPLE STORY THAT STUCK WITH ME

During my basketball career, I had a teammate who constantly encouraged me to push myself in practice, even on drills I thought I had mastered. At the time, I didn't think much of it.

Years later, when I became a leader in business, I found myself encouraging my own team in the same way. That teammate's habit had become part of my leadership DNA without me even realizing it.

That's the ripple. It keeps going, even when the original source is long gone.

THE 1% PUSH MULTIPLIER EFFECT

One leader giving one push a day can influence a handful of people. But if each of those people starts giving "pushes" of their own, the growth multiplies exponentially.

In math terms, it's not addition; it's compound interest.

> **LOCKER ROOM LESSON**
> *Your greatest impact as a leader isn't in what you achieve,*
> *it's in what you inspire others to achieve long after you're gone.*

REFLECTION QUESTIONS

1. Which of your past 1% pushes have had a ripple effect you've noticed?
2. How can you encourage your team to pay forward the pushes they've received?
3. What legacy do you want your leadership to leave?

ACTION STEPS

- Identify one team member who's ready to "pay it forward." Mentor them in giving their own 1% pushes.
- Share a story with your team about a ripple effect you've witnessed to inspire them.
- Make "pass it on" part of your team culture. When someone receives a push, they commit to giving one to someone else.

REAL LIFE STORY: THE HANDSHAKE THAT MEANT MORE THAN THE TROPHY

Years after I'd retired from basketball, I went to watch a game in which one of my former teammates, someone I had mentored when he was just starting out, was now coaching his own team.

This was the championship final for him. His team had been the underdog all season, but they played with heart, discipline, and confidence. And in the final moments of the game, when the score was close, I recognized one of the plays we used to run together, except now, he was the one calling it from the sidelines.

They won. The crowd roared. The players lifted him on their shoulders.

After the celebration died down, he spotted me in the stands, walked over, and shook my hand. He said, "You taught me how to believe I could do this. Tonight, I just passed that belief to them."

THE LEADERSHIP LESSON

The true measure of leadership isn't how many personal wins you rack up; it's how many people you've equipped to create wins of their own. When the people you develop go on to succeed, it creates a level of fulfillment deeper than titles or awards. There is a unique sense of pride that comes from knowing you played an active role in their growth and success, and that your impact continues long after your direct involvement.

Your legacy isn't the points you score; it's the players you've prepared to score without you.

TAKEAWAY FOR LEADERS

The legacy of a leader is measured in the victories of others. When you see someone you've mentored achieve their own success, you're not just witnessing a win; you're seeing your leadership in action.

Key Takeaway: The ripple effect of the 1% Push is how small acts of leadership turn into lasting cultural change. You may never see the full extent of your influence, but rest assured, it's spreading further than you think.

CHAPTER 10
BUILDING A CULTURE OF CONTINUOUS IMPROVEMENT

The difference between a good team and a great team is not talent; it's the commitment to keep getting better, even when things are going well.

In sports, this is the team that reviews film after a win, that runs sprints when they're already in shape, that works on free throws when they've just hit 90% in a game. They understand that improvement is never "done."

In business, it's the leader who says: We're proud of our results, but we're not done growing. That's the foundation of a culture of continuous improvement, the belief that no matter how good you are, you can always get better.

In a world that changes this fast, standing still means falling behind. Markets evolve, competitors adapt, and customer expectations shift constantly. A culture of continuous improvement ensures that you stay relevant in changing conditions, attract people who value growth and innovation, and build resilience by continually adjusting to challenges.

THE OFF-SEASON CHAMPIONS

Some of the best players I knew were not the most talented. They were the ones who dominated the off-season. They didn't just maintain their skills; they expanded them. They returned every season with something new in their game, a better three-point shot, a stronger left hand, and improved conditioning.

That's what organizations must do, every "off-season" (or project cycle), they should come back stronger, smarter, and more prepared.

THE 1% PUSH APPLIED TO CULTURE

The beauty of the 1% Push is that it scales, from individuals to entire teams to organizations.

At the cultural level, it means embedding habits and systems that make improvement part of daily operations, not just a reaction to problems.

Examples:

- Every team meeting includes a quick discussion on "one thing we can improve."
- Quarterly reviews include recognition for both results and innovations.
- Leaders regularly share lessons learned from both successes and failures.

A CORPORATE STORY

When I joined a global division in my corporate career, they had strong results but flat growth. People were comfortable, maybe too comfortable.

I introduced a small cultural 1% Push: every project post-mortem had to include one innovation we'd try next time. At first, it felt forced. But within six months, teams were competing to see who could come up with the most creative improvement.

Revenue grew. Morale improved. And the culture shifted from "good enough" to "how can we be better?"

FRAMEWORK: THE GROW CULTURE MODEL

- **G – Goals that stretch:** Set targets that push the team slightly beyond comfort.
- **R – Regular reflection:** Build in structured review points to learn from experience.
- **O – Open feedback:** Create a safe space where ideas and critiques are welcomed.
- **W – Win recognition:** Celebrate not just outcomes, but the efforts to improve.

THE ROLE OF LEADERSHIP

Leaders set the tone for continuous improvement by modeling curiosity and humility ("I don't know the answer, but let's find out"), admitting mistakes and showing what was learned, and rewarding initiative even when the result isn't perfect. If the leader treats improvement as optional, so will the team.

The best coaches design practices that simulate real-game pressure. That way, improvement isn't just theoretical; it's tested in conditions as close as possible to reality.

In business, that means running pilots, role-playing client conversations, or stress-testing new systems before going live.

OVERCOMING THE RESISTANCE

Continuous improvement can be uncomfortable because it often requires change, and people naturally resist change. The key is to start small: implement one improvement at a time, involve the team in choosing what to improve, and show quick wins to prove it is worth the effort.

THE 1% PUSH FOR CULTURE CHANGE

If your organization isn't used to improvement as a norm, start with micro-shifts:

- Replace "We've always done it this way" with "What could make this even better?"
- Encourage one experiment per quarter in each department.
- Share success stories of small changes that had big impacts.

When we started embracing micro-shifts like these, the culture began to change. Teams that used to resist new ideas started suggesting their own improvements. Small experiments led to smarter processes, faster collaboration, and greater ownership. Within a few months, "We've always done it this way" turned into "What if we tried this?" That mindset shift, one small push at a time, created measurable progress and a culture where improvement became the norm, not the exception.

A RIPPLE STORY AT SCALE

In one company I coached, a single customer service rep suggested changing the greeting script to make it more conversational. The change was tiny, a few words.

But it improved customer satisfaction scores, which led to better reviews, which led to more referrals. That small improvement sparked a ripple effect across the company's bottom line.

> **LOCKER ROOM LESSON**
> *Great teams aren't built in the spotlight; they're built in the daily grind of getting better.*

REFLECTION QUESTIONS

1. Does your current culture reward maintenance or improvement?
2. Where in your processes do you have space for regular reflection and learning?
3. What's one cultural 1% Push you could start this month?

ACTION STEPS

- Choose one recurring meeting to include a "1% improvement" agenda item.
- Identify and share a story of a small improvement that had a big payoff.
- Recognize one person publicly for their contribution in making something better.

REAL LIFE STORY: THE CALL FROM AN OLD TEAMMATE

A few years after my basketball career ended, I got a phone call from one of my former teammates. We hadn't spoken in years, but he was excited. His company had just closed a massive deal, one that would completely change his career trajectory.

He said, "You know, I used a lot of what you taught me back when we played together. I remembered how you'd always make me run that extra drill, how you'd pull me aside after games and point out one thing I could improve on. I didn't realize it at the time, but you were teaching me more than basketball. You were teaching me how to push myself, even when nobody's watching."

I hung up the phone that day with a bigger sense of pride than I ever had after scoring a winning basket. Because this wasn't my win; it was his. And knowing that something I had invested years ago was still paying dividends in someone else's life... that's when I understood what legacy really means.

The Leadership Lesson

The real legacy of leadership lives in the skills, mindset, and confidence you leave in the people who will one day lead without you.

> *The real scoreboard of leadership isn't in today's points,*
> *it's in tomorrow's wins you'll never play in.*

TAKEAWAY FOR LEADERS

Your greatest victories are often invisible in the moment but monumental in the long run. Invest in people so deeply that when they succeed on their own, they carry a piece of your leadership with them.

Key Takeaway: A culture of continuous improvement doesn't happen by accident. It's built intentionally, with consistent 1% pushes that make progress a habit rather than a rare event.

CHAPTER 11
LEADING THROUGH CHANGE

Change is the one constant in leadership. Markets shift. Technology evolves. Strategies adapt. And no matter how much we plan, change rarely arrives on our schedule.

The challenge isn't whether change will come; it's how you and your team will respond when it does.

Humans are wired for comfort. We like patterns, predictability, and control. Change disrupts all three. That's why even positive change, like a promotion or a big win, can cause stress.

In leadership, your role during change is twofold:

1. Stabilize the team by providing clarity and confidence.
2. Mobilize the team to take action despite uncertainty.

SPORTS ANALOGY: THE HALFTIME ADJUSTMENT

In basketball, no matter how good your game plan is, by halftime, the other team has made adjustments. That's when great coaches shine.

They read the situation, tweak the strategy, and rally the team to execute a new plan.

The best coaches don't panic. They explain the "why" behind the changes, give clear instructions, and remind the team they have what it takes to win.

That's exactly what leaders must do in business during times of change.

THE ROLE OF THE 1% PUSH IN CHANGE

When the future feels uncertain, people often freeze. The 1% Push breaks that paralysis by focusing on small, manageable actions that move the team forward.

Examples:

- Instead of overhauling the entire sales process at once, introduce one new client question this week.
- Instead of launching a new system in every department, pilot it with one team.
- Instead of demanding an immediate culture shift, start with one behavior to adopt now.

These small pushes reduce fear, build momentum, and make change feel achievable.

A CORPORATE STORY

When my company went through a major restructure, I saw two types of leaders: those who waited for all the answers before taking action and those who guided their teams forward with small, clear steps. One leader in particular stood out. She didn't sugarcoat the uncertainty, but she told her team, "Here's what we know. Here's what we can control this week. Let's focus on that." That 1% Push mindset kept her team engaged and productive while others stalled.

FRAMEWORK: THE CHANGE MODEL

- **C – Clarify the "Why":** Explain the reason for the change so people see the bigger picture.
- **H – Highlight the Positives:** Identify opportunities and benefits.
- **A – Acknowledge Concerns:** Address fears without dismissing them.
- **N – Narrow the Focus:** Identify small, actionable steps.
- **G – Guide and Support:** Provide resources and encouragement.
- **E – Evaluate and Adjust:** Learn from early actions and refine the approach.

In sports, mistakes happen: A turnover, a missed shot, a bad call, but you can't stay stuck there. You have to focus on the next play.

In change management, the "next play" mentality keeps teams from dwelling on what's lost and instead focuses them on what's next.

BALANCING EMPATHY AND ACCOUNTABILITY DURING CHANGE

This is where empathetic accountability becomes critical: pair empathy (recognizing that change is stressful and people process it at different speeds) with accountability(reminding the team that the mission still matters and the work must continue). If you lean too far into empathy without accountability, performance drops; lean too far into accountability without empathy, and you lose trust.

THE 1% PUSH FOR THE LEADER

Leading through change is exhausting, which means you also need to push yourself. That might mean seeking perspective from a mentor, staying disciplined with routines that keep you grounded, and limiting the time you spend focusing on things you cannot control.

Here is a ripple-effect story. During a merger, one manager I knew started every team meeting with this question: "What's one thing we can do today to move forward?" At first, the answers were small, such as replying to client emails faster or connecting with a colleague in another department. But over time, the habit built momentum, and the team became known as the most adaptable group in the company. Her simple daily question became part of the culture long after she left.

> **LOCKER ROOM LESSON**
> *You don't have to control the storm.*
> *You just have to keep the ship moving.*

REFLECTION QUESTIONS

1. How do you currently lead during uncertainty with calm clarity or reactive urgency?
2. What's one 1% Push you can give your team right now to adapt to a change you're facing?
3. How can you balance empathy and accountability in your communication?

ACTION STEPS

- Identify one aspect of the current change you can control, and communicate it clearly to your team.
- Break the change into small, manageable steps and assign ownership.
- Schedule a regular "evaluate and adjust" session to keep improving as you adapt.

REAL LIFE STORY: THE YEAR EVERYTHING CHANGED

One season during my basketball journey, our team underwent a massive shake-up: new coach, new playbook, and new roles for almost everyone. Overnight, everything we'd been comfortable with was gone.

At first, it was chaos. Players were frustrated. Practices felt like we were starting from scratch. Some wanted to cling to the old ways; others wanted to overhaul everything immediately.

Our coach pulled us into the locker room one day and said something I'll never forget:

"We're not going to survive this season by focusing on what's gone. We're going to win it by mastering what's in front of us: one drill, one play, one possession at a time."

So that's what we did. We didn't try to perfect the whole system in a week. We focused on small, daily adjustments: the 1% Push. We learned the new plays step by step, built trust in the new rotations, and adjusted to our coach's style little by little.

By the end of the season, not only had we adapted, but we were thriving. And we realized that the change we had feared so much had actually unlocked a better version of us.

THE LEADERSHIP LESSON

Change is uncomfortable because it forces us out of the familiar. But great leaders don't just weather change; they guide their teams through it by breaking it into manageable steps, maintaining trust, and keeping focus on progress rather than perfection.

In times of change, you don't win by leaping the mountain; you win by climbing it one step at a time.

TAKEAWAY FOR LEADERS

When leading through change, lead your team step by step, keep morale high, and celebrate each small win along the way. The 1% Push during change not only helps your team adapt, it helps them emerge stronger than before.

Key Takeaway: Leading through change is less about having all the answers and more about creating steady forward motion. With the 1% Push, you can help your team adapt, stay engaged, and even grow stronger through the process.

CHAPTER 12
THE LEADER'S MINDSET: PLAYING THE LONG GAME

Anyone can have a good week. A few can have a good year. But great leaders? They create a track record of success that spans seasons, cycles, and challenges.

They know the secret to sustained leadership impact isn't in dramatic sprints, it's in consistent, disciplined effort over time. And that's exactly what the 1% Push was made for.

In business and sports alike, early success can be misleading. A team can go on a hot streak but fade when injuries or fatigue set in, and a company can have a breakthrough product but fail to innovate after the initial buzz.

Long-game leaders are different: they stay relevant by adapting without losing their core principles, keep their teams motivated even when results take time, and build legacies that outlast them.

THE CAREER OF A CHAMPION

Think of athletes like Serena Williams, Tom Brady, or LeBron James. Their greatness isn't defined by a single season; it's defined by sustained excellence over decades.

How do they do it?

- They take care of their bodies year-round.
- They adapt their game as they age.
- They never stop studying and refining their craft.

In leadership, the same principles apply. You can't rely on what worked five years ago. You have to evolve, maintain your energy, and keep learning.

THE 1% PUSH AS A LONG-GAME STRATEGY

The reason the 1% Push is so powerful for long-term leadership is that it is sustainable. Anyone can grind at one hundred ten percent for a short period, but that pace leads to burnout. Small, daily pushes build momentum without draining your energy. Over time, they compound, much like compound interest in investing.

Take learning, for example. A leader who reads ten pages of a leadership book each day will finish twelve to fifteen books a year. A leader who chooses to recognize one person a week gradually builds a culture of appreciation that lasts. These habits do not require dramatic effort, but they create dramatic results.

The same applies to coaching. A leader who spends just five minutes a day giving targeted feedback builds a team that improves in real time. Those small, consistent moments of guidance create clarity, confidence, and accountability. Eventually, the team stops waiting to be corrected and begins self-correcting, taking ownership of their growth and performance.

Similarly, a leader who schedules one coffee chat a week with someone outside their immediate team strengthens collaboration across the organization. Those simple conversations build trust, break down silos, and often spark new ideas. What starts as a connection turns into culture, proof that meaningful relationships are the foundation of long-term success.

A CORPORATE STORY

I once worked with a division head who took over a struggling department. Instead of overhauling everything at once, he made small, steady changes:

- **Month 1:** Improving onboarding shortened ramp-up time and boosted confidence; new hires became productive faster because they understood expectations, culture, and resources from day one.
- **Month 2:** Increasing the frequency of feedback sessions created momentum. Instead of waiting for quarterly reviews, people adjusted and improved in real time. Performance gaps closed quickly, and engagement scores began to rise.
- **Month 3:** Introducing cross-team collaboration meetings broke down silos and unlocked innovation. Departments began sharing best practices, solving problems faster, and supporting each other's goals. Productivity improved, but more importantly, so did morale. The team started performing like one connected unit instead of separate groups.

Two years later, the division was outperforming every other region, and the culture was stronger than ever. He played the long game, and it paid off.

The turnaround happened because he focused on consistency, not quick fixes. Instead of overhauling everything at once, he built trust first, listening to his team, setting clear expectations, and following through on every commitment. Over time, that consistency created belief, and belief drove performance. People stopped working for him and started working with him. That's when results and culture began to compound.

FRAMEWORK: THE PACE FORMULA FOR SUSTAINABLE LEADERSHIP

- **P – Prioritize Energy:** Protect your mental, physical, and emotional stamina. Leaders can't pour from an empty cup.
- **A – Adapt Strategically:** Be willing to pivot while holding onto your core values.
- **C – Commit to Consistency:** Small actions repeated daily outpace occasional big moves.
- **E – Expand Capacity:** Invest in your people so you're not the only driver of performance.

SPORTS ANALOGY: SEASON VS. CAREER

A coach once told me, "Anyone can survive a season. But can you build a career?"

Leaders who only focus on the "season," the next quarter's results, often make decisions that sacrifice long-term success for short-term gains. Long-game leaders think in years, not months.

That means developing people, protecting culture, and avoiding burnout for themselves and their teams.

THE ROLE OF RESILIENCE

Playing the long game isn't just about strategy; it's about resilience. You'll face setbacks, failures, and moments of doubt. Resilient leaders view setbacks as lessons rather than verdicts, stay grounded in their purpose when circumstances change, and lean on trusted peers, mentors, and routines to regain momentum.

THE 1% PUSH FOR YOURSELF AS A LONG-GAME LEADER

Your own pushes might include:

- Blocking thirty minutes a week for reflection and strategic thinking.
- Investing in leadership development courses annually.
- Building personal rituals that keep you grounded during high-pressure seasons.

> **LOCKER ROOM LESSON**
> *Success isn't won in a single game; it's built across seasons of consistent play.*

REFLECTION QUESTIONS

1. Are your current leadership decisions serving the season or the career?
2. How can you apply the 1% Push to your own growth as a leader?
3. What will your leadership legacy look like five or ten years from now?

ACTION STEPS

- Choose one long-term investment you'll make in yourself or your team this year.
- Identify and eliminate one habit that drains your energy without adding value.
- Create a "legacy list," actions you can take now to build the culture you want to leave behind.

REAL LIFE STORY: THE SEASON THAT WASN'T ABOUT THIS SEASON

One season, I played on a rebuilding team. We had talent, but we were rebuilding, with too many rookies, too many new plays, and too much change all at once.

Some players checked out early, just going through the motions. But our coach had a different approach. He sat us down and said:

"We're not playing for the trophy this year. We're building the team that's going to win it next year."

That shifted everything. Suddenly, every practice mattered, not because of this weekend's game, but because of what we'd be able to do a year from now. Every 1% improvement we made in fitness, communication, and trust was an investment in our future success.

Sure enough, the following year, we came back stronger, more connected, and ready to dominate. And we did.

THE LEADERSHIP LESSON

True leaders don't just chase short-term wins; they set their sights on sustained success. Playing the long game means making strategic decisions today that may not pay off immediately, but build the foundation for something far greater.

Championships aren't built in a season;
they're built in the seasons before.

TAKEAWAY FOR LEADERS

Don't let short-term pressures blind you to long-term opportunities. When you play the long game, you teach your team to value growth over quick wins, and to see every challenge as an investment in their future.

Key Takeaway: The 1% Push isn't just a performance booster; it's a leadership philosophy built for the long game. By pacing yourself, adapting, and staying consistent, you can lead with impact for years to come.

CHAPTER 13
DEVELOPING LEADERS WHO GIVE THE 1% PUSH

The true measure of your leadership isn't just in what you achieve, it's in the leaders you develop along the way.

It's one thing to be the person giving the 1% Push. It's another to build a team of leaders who can give it to themselves, multiplying your influence far beyond your personal reach.

This is how legacies are built, not by the size of your own results, but by the number of leaders who carry your philosophy into the future.

WHY MULTIPLYING LEADERS MATTERS

When only you give the Push, your reach is limited to the number of people you directly influence. But when you grow other leaders who give the push, your culture becomes self-sustaining, performance improvements happen organically, and innovation spreads faster because more people feel empowered to lead. This isn't leadership addition; it's leadership multiplication.

THE PLAYER-COACH EFFECT

On every great sports team, there are players who act like coaches on the floor. They call out plays, encourage teammates, and hold others accountable, even though they're not the official leader.

As a pro basketball player, I loved playing with "player-coaches" because they extended the coach's influence during the game.

In business, these "player-coaches" are your emerging leaders, and your job is to find them, develop them, and empower them to give their own 1% pushes.

THE 1% PUSH AS A TEACHABLE SKILL

The Push isn't just an instinct; it's a skill you can teach:

- **Spot the Moment** – Recognizing when someone is ready for a small stretch.
- **Deliver with Care** – Framing the challenge so it motivates instead of intimidates.
- **Follow Through** – Supporting the person after the Push to help them succeed.

By breaking this down into a repeatable process, you make it something others can master.

A CORPORATE STORY

I once led a team where one member stood out for his natural influence on others. He wasn't in a leadership role, but people gravitated to him.

I started mentoring him on the 1% Push, showing him how to identify moments to challenge others, how to balance encouragement with accountability, and how to debrief after the push.

Within a year, he had stepped into a formal leadership role. But more importantly, he was developing his own leaders, and the cycle continued.

FRAMEWORK: THE MENTOR MODEL FOR DEVELOPING LEADERS

- **M – Model It:** Demonstrate the 1% Push in your daily actions so they see it in practice.
- **E – Explain It:** Share the philosophy and mechanics behind it. Don't assume they "just get it."
- **N – Notice Potential:** Identify people who naturally influence others, even without a title.
- **T – Train with Real Scenarios:** Use role-plays, case studies, and live coaching moments.
- **O – Offer Feedback:** Give constructive guidance as they try giving their own pushes.
- **R – Recognize Progress:** Celebrate when they use the push effectively, reinforcing the behavior.

PASSING THE PLAYBOOK

A team's playbook contains its winning strategies. Great coaches pass the playbook to assistant coaches, captains, and future leaders so the system stays alive even when the head coach leaves.

In leadership, your 1% Push philosophy is your playbook. Pass it down intentionally, and you'll see it thrive long after you've moved on.

OVERCOMING THE FEAR OF DELEGATED LEADERSHIP

Some leaders hesitate to grow other leaders because they worry about losing control, relevance, or authority. But the truth is that developing leaders makes you more valuable, not less; your influence grows when your people succeed; and the leaders you grow ultimately reflect the quality of your own leadership.

THE RIPPLE EFFECT AT SCALE

When you develop leaders who give the Push:

- One leader impacts five people.
- Those five become leaders, impacting twenty-five.
- Over time, the reach becomes exponential.

This is how movements are built.

THE 1% PUSH FOR YOURSELF AS A LEADER DEVELOPER

Your personal 1% Push could be to identify one potential leader each quarter to mentor, allow an emerging leader to take the lead on a project while you coach from the sidelines, and share your own leadership mistakes openly so they learn faster.

A RIPPLE STORY

Years ago, I mentored a young leader who initially lacked confidence. Through consistent 1% pushes, I asked her to lead a small meeting, present to leadership, and eventually run a full initiative. She transformed.

Today, she leads a large team, and I've seen her use the same 1% Push approach with her people. That's when you know your leadership has multiplied.

> **LOCKER ROOM LESSON**
> *The greatest leaders don't just build teams;*
> *they build leaders who build teams.*

REFLECTION QUESTIONS

1. Who on your team shows natural leadership influence, even without a title?
2. How intentionally are you teaching others to give the 1% Push?
3. What systems could you put in place to keep leader development ongoing?

ACTION STEPS

- Choose one person to begin mentoring on the 1% Push this month.
- Share a story with your team about how a leader once pushed you and how it shaped you.
- Create a mini "push challenge" where team members give a small Push to someone else and share the result.

REAL LIFE STORY: THE CAPTAIN WHO CREATED CAPTAINS

Late in my basketball career, I played alongside a team captain who had no interest in being the star player. He could have taken the final shot, called every play, and been the center of attention, but instead, he made it his mission to create other leaders on the team.

He'd pull younger players aside after practice and say, "Tomorrow, you're running the warm-up drills." If a game was tight, he'd sometimes hand the ball to a less experienced player, saying, "This is your moment. Take it."

At first, it felt risky. Giving responsibility to someone untested could cost us the game. But over time, something incredible happened. The entire team became confident in making decisions, not just following them.

By the end of the season, we had multiple players capable of stepping up as leaders. And when our captain retired, the transition was seamless because he'd been building his replacements all along.

THE LEADERSHIP LESSON

The most impactful leaders don't just create results; they create other leaders who can deliver results without them. The 1% Push isn't just for performance; it's a tool to develop leadership confidence in others, one decision and one opportunity at a time.

The best leaders don't just take the shot;
they teach others how to take it.

TAKEAWAY FOR LEADERS

If you want your leadership to outlast you, give others the space, encouragement, and trust to lead, even if it means stepping back so they can step forward.

Key Takeaway: Your legacy as a leader is not just in what you achieve, but in the leaders you leave behind. When you teach others to give the 1% Push, you create a ripple effect that can last generations.

CHAPTER 14
THE COMMON PITFALLS OF THE 1% PUSH (AND HOW TO AVOID THEM)

When used well, the 1% Push is one of the most powerful leadership tools you'll ever have.

When used poorly, it can backfire, leading to frustration, disengagement, or even turnover.

The difference between success and failure often comes down to how you deliver the Push, when you deliver it, and why you deliver it.

Most pitfalls aren't the result of bad intentions; they happen because we confuse pushing with pressuring, we fail to consider timing or context, and we make it about our agenda rather than their growth. Think of it like sports: the right drill at the wrong time can cause injury, and the wrong drill at the right time still wastes the moment.

OVERTRAINING VS. SMART TRAINING

In professional sports, overtraining is real. Athletes who push too hard without recovery time get injured or burned out.

In leadership, over-pushing can cause the same thing: mental fatigue, reduced motivation, and resentment. The 1% Push is meant to stretch, not strain.

PITFALL #1: THE "TOO MUCH, TOO SOON" PUSH

Some leaders see potential and immediately go into overdrive. They pile on new responsibilities, stretch goals, and constant feedback.

The Problem:

- The person feels overwhelmed instead of inspired.

The Fix:

- Start small: one new challenge at a time.
- Check in frequently to assess capacity.
- Build wins before raising the bar again.

Example: Instead of asking a new team member to lead a major project right away, have them run one segment of a meeting. Let them build confidence in stages.

Early in my corporate leadership journey, I saw potential in a new hire and immediately loaded her up with responsibilities. Within weeks, she was exhausted, not because she lacked ability, but because she lacked wins. I pulled back, gave her ownership of one client meeting segment, and coached her through it. She crushed it. From there, we built gradually, one challenge at a time. Within six months, she was confidently managing full accounts.

Outcome: Confidence through consistency, not overload.

PITFALL #2: THE "ONE-SIZE-FITS-ALL" PUSH

What motivates one person can demotivate another. Giving the same type of push to everyone ignores their unique personalities, strengths, and goals.

The Problem:

- The push feels impersonal, or worse, irrelevant.

The Fix:

- Know your people: What drives them, what scares them, and what excites them.
- Tailor the push to match their current capabilities and aspirations.

Example: A sprinter and a long-distance runner both train hard, but their programs look completely different.

I once motivated two team members in completely different ways, one thrived under public recognition, the other preferred quiet one-on-one acknowledgment. When I tried to motivate both the same way, I lost their engagement. I adjusted by learning what truly drove each of them; one wanted visibility, and the other valued growth opportunities.

Outcome: Tailored motivation led to higher engagement and stronger results from both individuals.

PITFALL #3: THE "NO SAFETY NET" PUSH

Some leaders think the push is enough on its own. They challenge someone but don't provide support, feedback, or resources.

The Problem:

- The person struggles unnecessarily, possibly failing in a way that damages confidence.

The Fix:

- Pair every push with guidance and access to tools or coaching.
- Make it clear you're there to help them succeed.

Example: I once asked a new manager to lead a regional rollout without giving her access to resources she needed. She worked hard but felt unsupported and frustrated. After seeing her struggle, I stepped in not to take over but to coach her through stakeholder management and connect her to the right tools.

Outcome: With support, she not only delivered the rollout successfully but became a go-to leader for future initiatives.

PITFALL #4: THE "SILENT PUSH"

Sometimes leaders challenge someone but never explain why. Without the context, it can feel like busywork or even punishment.

The Problem:

- The growth opportunity is missed because the purpose isn't clear.

The Fix:

- Always connect the push to their growth and the bigger mission.
- Use language that frames it as an opportunity, not a chore.

Example: I once reassigned a project to a senior team member as a growth opportunity, but I never explained why. He took it as criticism, not trust. When I clarified that I chose him because I believed he could elevate it, his mindset flipped; he went from defensive to driven.

Outcome: Clear intent turned resistance into ownership.

PITFALL #5: THE "NEVER FOLLOW-UP" PUSH

A push without follow-up is like a pass without looking to see if your teammate caught the ball.

The Problem:

- The person doesn't get feedback, reinforcement, or recognition, so the impact fades.

The Fix:

- Circle back quickly: Celebrate progress, address challenges, and set the next step.

Example: I once challenged a rising leader to improve her presentation skills and gave her full freedom to prepare. She did the work, but I failed to follow up after the meeting. Later, she told me she wasn't sure if her effort even mattered. That was a wake-up call. I made it a habit to circle back quickly, acknowledge progress, give feedback, and set the next challenge.

Outcome: Quick follow-ups created momentum, trust, and sustained growth.

Together, these experiences reinforced one truth: the 1% Push only works when challenge and support move together.

FRAMEWORK: THE SAFE PUSH METHOD

To avoid these pitfalls, use the SAFE method:

- **S – Specific:** Tailor the push to the individual.
- **A – Actionable:** Make it clear what the next step is.
- **F – Follow-Up:** Check in to guide and reinforce.
- **E – Encouraging:** Deliver it in a way that inspires confidence, not fear.

A CORPORATE STORY

A senior manager I coached was eager to help her team grow, but she kept losing people to burnout. She realized she was piling too many changes on too quickly. We redesigned her approach by focusing on one development push per quarter for each team member, providing clear context for why it mattered, and scheduling check-ins at the halfway point. Retention improved, performance increased, and, most importantly, trust deepened.

A senior manager I coached wanted to help her team grow, but couldn't understand why turnover kept rising. The issue wasn't intent; it was pace. She was giving her people too many pushes at once, leaving them overwhelmed instead of motivated. Together, we redesigned her approach: one focused Push per quarter, clear context for why it mattered, and mid-cycle check-ins for support. Within six months, burnout dropped, retention improved by nearly 30%, and overall performance metrics rose across the board. But the biggest shift wasn't in the numbers; it was in trust. Her team no longer feared growth; they started asking for it.

THE RIGHT DRILL AT THE RIGHT TIME

A great coach doesn't just push players harder; they push smarter. They know when the team needs conditioning, when they need technical skills, and when they need recovery.

As a leader, your timing and precision matter just as much as your intensity.

THE EMOTIONAL SIDE OF PITFALLS

When the push goes wrong, it is not just performance that suffers; relationships can be damaged. If the push feels like pressure, trust erodes. If it feels impersonal, engagement drops. If it feels unsupported, confidence fades. The good news is that most of these issues can be prevented with intentional communication and empathy.

I once challenged a team member to take on a stretch project without realizing she was already overloaded. What I intended as an opportunity felt like pressure. Her performance slipped, and so did our trust. I learned that how I frame the push matters just as much as the push itself.

Another time, I rolled out the same development plan to my entire team. It was efficient, but impersonal. Some thrived; others disengaged. After one honest conversation, I realized each person needed something different. One wanted visibility, another needed structure, and another looked for creative freedom. Once I tailored my approach, motivation and results both climbed.

And I've seen what happens when a push lacks support. Early in my career, a leader handed me a major responsibility but disappeared when I needed guidance. I delivered, but barely, and my confidence took a hit. That experience shaped how I lead today: I never push someone without standing beside them through the process.

The good news? Every one of these missteps can be prevented with clear communication and empathy. When people understand the "why," feel seen as individuals, and know they're supported, the push doesn't create pressure; it creates progress.

THE 1% PUSH WITH ACCOUNTABILITY

Avoiding pitfalls doesn't mean avoiding accountability. You can still hold high standards; just do it in a way that leaves the person feeling supported, not abandoned.

Example: Instead of saying, "I need you to hit this target by next week," try, "I believe you can hit this target by next week. Let's meet on Wednesday to make sure you have what you need."

REFLECTION QUESTIONS

1. Which of these pitfalls have you fallen into before?
2. Who on your team might be at risk of feeling over-pushed right now?
3. How can you improve the balance between challenge and support?

ACTION STEPS

- Review the SAFE method before giving your next push.
- Ask for feedback from someone you've recently pushed. What worked and what didn't?
- Commit to one follow-up action for every push you give this month.

REAL LIFE STORY: WHEN MORE PUSH BECAME A PULL BACK

During one season, our coach bought into the idea of small, daily improvements, but somewhere along the way, "small" turned into too much.

At first, the changes were inspiring. A new drill here, a tweak to a play there. But then, every day felt like a new overhaul. Players didn't have time to master one adjustment before another was introduced. Instead of building confidence, the constant shifting caused frustration. Performance dipped, not because the ideas were bad, but because the team never had time to settle into them.

One day in practice, our point guard finally spoke up: "Coach, I can't even remember the first thing you wanted us to fix this week, because we're already on the third."

That was the turning point. The coach realized that the 1% Push works only when it's consistent, deliberate, and digestible, not when it becomes an avalanche of micro-demands. He scaled back, letting us master one small improvement before moving on to the next. Within weeks, the energy returned, and so did the results.

THE LEADERSHIP LESSON

The 1% Push fails when:

- It becomes the 10% push, too much change, too fast.
- There's no time to celebrate wins; momentum needs recognition.

A push that's too big stops being progress;
it becomes pressure.

TAKEAWAY FOR LEADERS

How to Avoid the Pitfalls:

- Prioritize: Focus on one key improvement at a time.
- Communicate the "Why": Tie each push to the bigger vision.
- Allow Mastery: Give your team space to fully absorb the change before adding the next.

Key Takeaway: The 1% Push is a precision tool, not a blunt instrument. When you avoid the common pitfalls and deliver it with timing, care, and clarity, it becomes one of the most effective ways to grow people without losing them.

CHAPTER 15
YOUR LEADERSHIP LEGACY: LIVING THE 1% PUSH

At the end of the day, and at the end of your career, leadership is not measured by titles, paychecks, or the number of meetings you ran.

It's measured by the impact you leave behind.

The people you developed.

The culture you created.

The moments when people say, "I wouldn't be where I am without you."

That is your legacy.

And the 1% Push isn't just a leadership tactic, it's a legacy-building philosophy.

WHY LEGACY MATTERS

Legacy is proof that your influence outlives your presence. Projects will end, titles will change, and markets will shift. But the leaders you build, the confidence you inspire, and the growth you spark ripple far beyond your tenure.

Playing for legacy means thinking beyond immediate wins. You invest in people, knowing the returns may not fully appear until years later.

THE NUMBER IN THE RAFTERS

In sports, the highest honor isn't a trophy; it's having your jersey retired and your number hanging in the rafters. Why? Because that means you weren't just a good player; you were a transformative presence. The team, the fans, and the culture are forever better because you were part of it.

That's what the 1% Push can do for you as a leader. It gets your number "in the rafters" of your organization's history.

THE 1% PUSH AS A LIFESTYLE

When you live the 1% Push every day, you start looking for small moments to inspire growth in conversations, in feedback, and in decisions. You stay curious because every interaction could be a catalyst for change, and you create momentum that does not need you in the room to keep going. It becomes how you lead, not just something you do occasionally.

A CORPORATE STORY

One executive I worked with had an incredible retirement celebration. As people came to the microphone, almost every story started the same way:

"She gave me a chance I didn't think I deserved."

"She believed in me before I believed in myself."

That's the power of living the 1% Push over a career. It turns leadership into legacy.

Her impact wasn't measured in titles or revenue; it was measured in people. Dozens of careers and countless moments of confidence and growth existed because she chose to see potential before perfection. Her belief didn't just build a team; it built a legacy.

THE RIPPLE MULTIPLIED

Throughout this book, we've talked about the ripple effect: how one push can spark growth in someone who goes on to push others. By the time you retire, your legacy could be dozens of leaders giving their own pushes, a culture that outperforms because people challenge and support one another, and a reputation that makes people proud to say, "I worked with them."

Going back to the retirement celebration I just mentioned, one former employee shared how, early in her career, she'd made a major mistake that could've derailed her. Instead of being punished, her leader sat her down and said, "This isn't the end; it's your starting point. Let's learn from it." That moment changed the trajectory of her career. Another talked about being terrified to take on a leadership role, until her boss looked her in the eye and said, "You're ready. You just don't believe in yourself yet."

As the evening went on, it became clear that this wasn't just a farewell party. It was a sense of gratitude from people whose lives had been shaped by one leader's belief in them.

That's the power of living the 1% Push over a career. Small, consistent acts of belief, a conversation here, a challenge there, that compound into something far greater. They build leaders. They shape cultures. They turn success into significance.

That night reminded me of a simple truth: the greatest legacy a leader can leave isn't what they achieved, it's who they empowered.

FRAMEWORK: THE LEGACY APPROACH

- **L – Lead with Intent:** Every action has purpose. You're not just reacting.
- **E – Empower Others:** You grow leaders, not followers.
- **G – Give Consistently:** The push is part of your daily rhythm, not a special occasion.
- **A – Adapt and Evolve:** Legacy leaders stay relevant because they keep learning.
- **C – Celebrate Progress:** Recognize growth, not just results.
- **Y – Your Values, Always:** Your integrity is the foundation of your influence.

COACHING TREES

In the NBA and NFL, they talk about "coaching trees," the network of coaches who once worked under a legendary leader and went on to lead their own teams. An example is college basketball coaching legend John Wooden, who did not just win championships at UCLA; he also developed future coaches and leaders whose influence spread across college and professional basketball. His legacy was not only in banners but in the habits, standards, and character he instilled in the people he led.

Bill Walsh did the same in the NFL. When he transformed the San Francisco 49ers, he did it by teaching principles, systems, and standards that his assistants carried into head coaching roles across the league. The coaches who learned under him shaped entire franchises and eras of football, proving that great leadership does not stop with winning games. It creates leaders who win long after the original coach is gone.

That is your legacy: a tree of leaders whose roots trace back to you.

THE FINAL 1% PUSH: FOR YOU

Now that you've read this book, here's your Push: don't just close the last page and go back to business as usual. Identify one person this week who could benefit from a small push, and deliver it with clarity, care, and belief in their potential. Then do it again next week, and the week after. It's not the grand gestures that will define your legacy; it's the daily pushes.

A RIPPLE STORY

Years ago, I coached a young professional who was shy, unsure, and almost invisible in the company. Through small, consistent pushes: volunteering for a meeting, presenting a single slide, leading a short project, she grew into a confident leader.

Last year, she messaged me: *"I used your 1% Push with someone on my team today. They lit up. I think I get it now. This is how change really happens."*

That message is why I do this work. That's legacy.

> **LOCKER ROOM LESSON**
> *Titles fade, numbers change, but the impact you make on people... that's forever.*

REFLECTION QUESTIONS

1. What do you want people to say about you when you're no longer in the room?
2. Who can you start developing today so they can carry your influence forward?
3. How will you keep the 1% Push alive in your own leadership journey?

ACTION STEPS

- Write your "leadership eulogy," the speech you'd want someone to give about you at the end of your career.
- Identify two to three people you'll commit to developing over the next year.
- Share the 1% Push philosophy with your team and invite them to practice it.

REAL LIFE STORY: THE LETTER I DIDN'T EXPECT

A few months after moving on from one of my leadership roles, I received a handwritten letter from a former team member. We'd worked together for years, but I never thought much about the impact I had on them personally. I was just doing what I thought leaders should do: giving small nudges, setting high standards, and encouraging them to aim a little higher each day.

The letter read:

"Nick, I wanted to thank you for never letting me settle. Even when I thought I'd done enough, you'd push me just a little further, not to prove you were right, but to show me I could be more. I still use that mindset today, and I'm passing it on to my own team."

Reading those words hit me harder than any award or bonus ever could. It was a reminder that leadership is not just about the goals we hit while we're in the role, it's about the ripple effect we leave behind.

THE LEADERSHIP LESSON

You may never fully know the impact you've had on others until long after you've moved on. But the habits you instill, the belief you build, and the standards you set can continue to influence people for years, often in ways you can't measure.

> *The true measure of a leader is not the work they do,*
> *but the work that continues after they're gone.*

TAKEAWAY FOR LEADERS

The 1% Push isn't just a leadership method; it's a legacy. Live it daily, and one day you'll look back and realize that your real scoreboard is written in the growth of the people you've touched.

Final Takeaway: The 1% Push is more than a leadership tool. It's a way of living that ensures your influence will be felt long after you're gone. Small pushes, given consistently, build leaders. Leaders build cultures. Cultures change organizations. And organizations change the world.

> *The 1% Push isn't just how you lead,*
> *it's the legacy you leave.*

YOUR PUSH STARTS NOW

If you've made it to this page, you've already done something remarkable. You've invested in yourself as a leader. You've taken the time to reflect, learn, and prepare for the kind of leadership that changes people's lives.

But here's the truth: this book isn't the finish line. It's the starting whistle.

The 1% Push only works when it's lived daily. Not in grand, dramatic gestures, but in the small, intentional moments: the honest conversation you almost avoid but choose to have, the encouragement you offer when someone doubts themselves, the extra mile you walk beside your team even when you're tired.

One day, you'll look back and realize that the culture, confidence, and results you see around you were built in these moments. And that's when you'll know you've not just led; you've left a legacy.

So, go give that push. The next great leader is waiting for you to believe in them, challenge them, and help them see what they didn't think was possible. Because leadership isn't about how far you can go. It's about how far you can take others with you.

I'll be cheering you on. One push at a time.

— *Nick*

ABOUT THE AUTHOR

Nick Mornard is a former basketball player turned senior leader at a global Fortune 500 company, bestselling author of *Mindset is My Degree*, and the creator of the 1% Push leadership philosophy. With a career spanning international team leadership, coaching, and entrepreneurship, Nick's mission is to help leaders inspire performance without sacrificing people.

When he's not speaking on stages worldwide, coaching leaders, or running his travel agency, Nick co-hosts the Two for the Win podcast, bringing fresh perspectives on mindset, leadership, and growth.

ACKNOWLEDGMENTS

To the leaders who gave me room to grow, the teammates who pushed me forward, and the audiences who have embraced the 1% Push, you've been the reason I keep showing up with everything I've got.

Special thanks to my family and friends for believing in the mission, even when it meant late nights, early mornings, and endless sports analogies.

THE 1% PUSH RESOURCES

Ready to take The 1% Push from page to practice?

- Workshops & Keynotes – Bring The 1% Push to your leadership team or organization.
- Coaching Programs – One-on-one and group coaching to help leaders implement empowering accountability.
- Free Tools & Guides – Download leadership templates, reflection prompts, and playbooks at www.NickMornard.com.

STAY CONNECTED WITH NICK

Website: www.NickMornard.com

 LinkedIn: linkedin.com/in/nickmornard

 Instagram: www.instagram.com/niconomy

 Facebook: www.facebook.com/nicolas.mornard

Podcast: *Two for the Win* – Available on Spotify, Apple Podcasts, and YouTube.

ALSO BY NICK MORNARD

Mindset is My Degree: How to Harness a Growth Mindset to Achieve Your Full Potential in Leadership, Business, and Life.

THANK YOU FOR READING MY BOOK!

I'd love to connect and stay in touch!
Scan the QR Code:

I appreciate your interest in my book and value your feedback, as it helps me improve future versions. I would appreciate it if you could leave your invaluable review on Amazon.com with your feedback.
Thank you!

www.ingramcontent.com/pod-product-compliance
Lightning Source LLC
Chambersburg PA
CBHW022109090426
42743CB00008B/779